CAGNEY

Also by Michael Freedland:

Jolson

Irving Berlin

A BIOGRAPHY

by Michael Freedland

STEIN AND DAY/*Publishers*/New York

First published in 1975
Copyright © 1974 by Michael Freedland
Library of Congress Catalog Card No. 74-79424
All rights reserved
Designed by Ed Kaplin
Printed in the United States of America
Stein and Day/*Publishers*/Scarborough House, Briarcliff Manor, N. Y.
10510
ISBN 0-8128-1715-X

"Frisby and Doaks" by George M. Cohan
© 1942 by The New York Times Company. Reprinted by permission.

For my parents
—who started it all

ACKNOWLEDGMENTS

I first saw him with a derby hat over his eyes and a broad grin on his face in a picture called *The Strawberry Blonde*. I was a kid taken out to an evening film because my parents couldn't get a babysitter. A year or so later I saw him prancing across the stage singing about being a Yankee Doodle Dandy. It made an impression that didn't fade—so I had the advantage over the other Cagney watchers who imagined he was always a gangster pointing a finger and saying "You dirty rat." When it was revealed that James Cagney was to be given a special Life Achievement Award by the American Film Institute in 1974 I recalled the days when a trip to the cinema was the big, big treat and flew the Atlantic to do a series of short radio programs on James Cagney, the gangster who wanted to become a dancer. What I learned made me realize that there was too much to be confined to my original brief. This book is the result of meeting people like James Cagney himself, who gave me the privilege of one of a handful of interviews he has allowed in the past thirteen years, but who knew no more than I did at the time that it would result in this book, which I hope says a lot of the things he would find it difficult to say about himself.

So my first thanks are to him and to those other people in Hollywood who gave so freely of their time to talk about their pal Jim (or Jimmy). It was a marvelous experience because I was allowed to spend my time with people like Ralph Bellamy, Pat O'Brien and Eddie Foy, Jr., who with James Cagney himself have now enriched that recess in my brain labeled "memories." My thanks, too, to those other stars who were kind enough to talk to me: Edmond O'Brien, George Burns, George Raft, Jack Lemmon (who was as helpful, humorous and kind as he had been when we met before), Joan Blondell, Mr. Cagney's close friends A. C. Lyles and Serge Bongart (a man I should love to have teach me painting). Thanks, too, to Ivor Davis of the London *Daily Express* and to Dennis Sykes.

I also appreciate the help of the librarians at the Lincoln Center Library in New York and the British Museum Newspaper Library in London.

My very sincere thanks for her help and encouragement to my editor Michaela Hamilton and for the patience of my colleagues, particularly Joe Dray of the London *Evening Standard.*

I should also like to acknowledge with gratitude the permission given me by Sammy Cahn to quote his parody of the song "My Way" as rendered by Frank Sinatra at the American Film Institute presentation to James Cagney in March 1974.

—Michael Freedland

CONTENTS

1	THE IRISH IN US	11
2	ANGELS WITH DIRTY FACES	21
3	BOY MEETS GIRL	28
4	FOOTLIGHT PARADE	37
5	PICTURE SNATCHER	59
6	THE PUBLIC ENEMY	64
7	HARD TO HANDLE	80
8	STARLIFT	89
9	SHAKE HANDS WITH THE DEVIL	98
10	THE CROWD ROARS	103
11	CITY FOR CONQUEST	115
12	SMART MONEY	127
13	THE FIGHTING 69TH	142
14	YANKEE DOODLE DANDY	157
15	THE GALLANT HOURS	173
16	CEILING ZERO	189

This is not an authorized biography of James Cagney.

17	WHITE HEAT	194
18	WHAT PRICE GLORY?	201
19	SOMETHING TO SING ABOUT	207
20	A MIDSUMMER NIGHT'S DREAM	231
21	COME FILL THE CUP	239
22	JIMMY THE GENT	243
	INDEX	249

CAGNEY

1 THE IRISH IN US

JAMES FRANCIS CAGNEY was a beefy Irishman who drank more than was good for him—which perhaps was not surprising, since he worked as a bartender, with the smell of beer and whiskey constantly under his nostrils.

By all accounts, this Cagney was a handsome man with blue-black hair and an ambition to have his own saloon. Anyone listening to his brogue as he dispensed the drink at Comerford's on First Avenue would find it easy to believe that years before, in County Leitrim, his people had been known as the O'Caignes. Cagney was a sort of Americanization of the original.

In the same way, a Norwegian sea captain called Nelson had probably once used a more Scandinavian spelling for his own family name. He married an Irish lass and it was their daughter, Carolyn Nelson, who met and fell in love with the bartender James Cagney.

On New York's East Side, the Cagneys were married and set up home. Their neighbors were other Irish families, as well as the Jews and Italians who were also experiencing their first days as Americans.

Soon there was a third member of the family, a boy they called Harry. When their second son was born on July 17, 1899, they did what an Irish family might have been expected to do the first time around: they named the child after his father. James Francis Cagney, Jr., was born in the family apartment at the corner of Eighth Street and Avenue D. It was the Lower East Side all right, but Mrs. Cagney wouldn't hear of its being described as a slum. Seventy-five years later, neither would her son.

Objectively, though, the Cagneys' neighborhood was not the best part of New York, or even of the workingmen's East Side. Nor was it the best part of the city in which to be running a saloon—and for a man like James, who had now decided he had had enough of working for others, that was important.

In 1900, the Cagneys moved to the Upper East Side. Cagney, Sr., had achieved his ambition and was finally owner of his own saloon. It must have given him a feeling of pride when he kissed his beloved "Carrie," as he always called her, goodbye every morning. From the first day he stood by the door of the small new house on Seventy-ninth Street, just a few yards from First Avenue, until he was too ill to work any more, he never forgot that morning kiss. When two more sons, Edward and William, joined the family circle, he would blow a kiss to them, too, and this also became part of the never-changing family routine.

Nor was a kiss the only ritual Cagney, Sr., would observe each morning. Afterward, he would set his bowler hat firmly on his head and bless himself. The blessing was part of his religion, but he had perfected a way of doing it that plainly was not. In one movement, he was able to feel from the top of his waistcoat halfway down his trousers—just to make sure that all his buttons were done up.

The Cagneys had their troubles. Two other babies were born and died in infancy. In the saloon, James, Sr., found it easier to drink with his customers than to sell to them. After a year, he had to close his business and take a job working for someone else. He alternated between bartending and being a bookkeeper.

Cagney had a reputation as a spendthrift. But for as long as people have been interested in finding out whether it was true or not, his namesake son has been denying it. The older Cagney was easygoing. He would say that it was easier to lend a friend a dollar than to find excuses for not doing so. Certainly, he had enough friends to make it worthwhile to tell his sons when they went on errands, "Don't forget to tell 'em Jimmy Cagney sent you."

When he had a spare dollar it usually went on the horses or on liquor. But he always drank "quietly," as the younger Jimmy later put it. The only way the family would know if he had had too much to drink was by studying the angle at which he wore his hat. When it was pulled down sharply from left to right, it was clear he had had more than enough.

Cagney loved his family and when he could forget the problems that were constantly besetting him, he tried to bring as much fun as he could into the family circle. He was one of those Irishmen who believed that making the family close depended on making friends of his children. This he did by making the boys laugh—particularly when it looked as though he were going to punish them. He'd put his right hand at the back of a boy's neck and make a fist. Then, just as he seemed about to give the youngster a real whacking, he'd say threateningly: "Now if I thought you meant that. . . ." He probably went through the routine hundreds of times, but it always got an appreciative laugh.

There's not much doubt that among the patrons in the saloons where Mr. Cagney worked were the tough guys his son was later to portray on the screen. Some would as soon kill a fellow drinker as they would buy him a glass of whiskey. Others were peddling drugs. The small-timers were the ones selling a rough form of opium the locals called "hopheads." The big business, however, was in "nose candy"—cocaine. When the tough guys weren't drinking in bars, they were on the street. Young Jimmy would watch them as he walked to and from school. Sometimes, he was even sitting next to them in the classroom.

Two things about the cocaine addict struck Jimmy as very odd: his eyes were constantly on the ground, and he always walked in a hurry. As a hoofer, Jimmy would refer to this peculiar gait as a "hippety hop." Jimmy didn't realize it at the time, but even as a small child he was beginning to take note of the people around him.

The Cagney house was in the part of Manhattan known as Yorkville. Once primarily the German quarter, by now it was also home for Irish and Italian families, just as for years the Lower East Side had been. To young James Cagney, the sounds of Naples and the Eastern European ghettos must have seemed as natural as the pledge of allegiance he recited in school each morning.

Yorkville's German traditions were reflected in the names of the buildings and open spaces in the neighborhood; many, like Carl Schurz Park, were named for German-born worthies of the past. It was in that park that Cagney remembers seeing a boy running ahead of him with a knife stuck in his back. It was a tough neighborhood, but with the defenses of childhood the Cagney youngsters didn't realize how tough it was.

Probably before he understood what it meant, Jimmy learned to recognize a drug peddler who was also the local pimp—in Yorkville society, a better-known figure than the neighborhood priest or rabbi. Everything about him fascinated the Cagney boys as they watched him standing outside a rathskeller.

It was the area of First Avenue between Seventy-seventh and Seventy-eighth Streets, and the pimp was always wearing an electric-blue suit and a straw hat. He impressed the older local boys because there were always at least four girls visibly under his control. But that fact didn't impress Jimmy nearly as much as the man's mannerisms. Repeatedly, the pimp would hitch up his trousers and at the same time nervously twitch his head and shoulders. Then, for emphasis, he would spit.

Jimmy watched and absorbed the details. He liked the way the pimp would strike one fist with the other. It was as if the man were either having a seizure or going mad because his collar was too tight. Today Cagney insists that the world's finest mimics are still copying that small-time New York pimp, whom Jimmy last saw being chased down the street by an irate husband.

It wasn't the sort of environment that caring parents wanted for their children. Whenever possible, the Cagneys tried to expose their children to other ways of life. Jimmy, Jr., was seven years old the first day that his father hired a horse and carriage and took the family into the country. They were visiting the boys' great-aunt, their grandmother's sister, who lived in what today is the Flatbush section of Brooklyn, not far from Kennedy Airport.

Jimmy thought the fields were greener than anything he had seen outside the paint box he used at school. Birds actually sang overhead, and there were cows and sheep in the fields. Above all he was impressed by the evocative smell—the lingering aroma—of the manure-scented carriage seats. It was the beginning of a love affair that grew more intense as the years passed. From that moment on, there was just one place Jimmy Cagney yearned to be—on the farm. Other kids in his neighborhood were planning to be cops, or kill cops, or drive fire engines; Jimmy was going to be a farmer. Certainly, it is safe to surmise that in those early years of the twentieth century, the idea of being a movie star was as far from Jimmy's mind as the thought of one day being president.

Plenty of the kids living in Yorkville were hoodlums before they could start school. Cagney remembers others as "good boys, tough but good." They were the ones who were his closest friends—Pete Levy, Artie Klein, and others who glorified in names like "Pickie" Houlihan, "Brother" O'Mara, Jake Brodkin, and "Loggerhead" Quinlivan—and they went to his home because it was known as a good place for playing Wild West games. Jimmy had persuaded his mother to part with an old sheepskin rug. He cut a hole in it, and with one of his father's discarded hats he could turn himself into a combination of both horse and cowboy.

Young Jimmy was as fascinated by his friends' faces as he was by the personalities behind them, and the borders of his schoolbooks were covered with caricatures of his classmates. Sometimes when there wasn't room for a drawing, or when the teacher was too close for comfort, he would just sit and stare at a kid. When he got home, he'd do an impression of him. Jimmy had no idea that the pictures he was drawing both on paper and in his head were of the type of character who years later would be as familiar to film audiences as they were to him then.

The immigrant children in Jimmy's classroom and their parents had a rich language that couldn't be read in books or overheard in conversation. They used their hands as much as their voices, and it fascinated Jimmy to see what stories could be told with a movement of a wrist and a thrust of an index finger. It was perhaps the best lesson of all.

Most of the Yorkville boys knew how to handle their fists

better than they could ever handle a book, and Jimmy admitted that English lessons were something of a "blur" for him. Reading, though, was important, whatever the subject was. A good adventure story fascinated him. One day when Jimmy was about nine years old, he was sitting on the street reading a Wild West story when a friend came by. Seeing what he was reading, the friend shouted: "You read those things and you'll go round killing people!"

The incident didn't seem to have any great significance at the time, but some years later, when Jimmy read that the same friend had gone to the electric chair for killing a policeman, he remembered it vividly.

"He wasn't a tough boy," Cagney recalls. "He grew up in a neighborhood where there were tough goings-on. But we didn't consider him particularly tough." Even some of the boys who were tough guys *par excellence* didn't think of themselves as tough. They just did things their own way—"and ended up in the hoosegow, as we used to call it."

Mr. and Mrs. Cagney were strong enough to steer their boys off crime. But it wasn't easy. While her husband was out working, Carrie would do what she could to broaden her children's minds. When she realized her second son was constantly thinking about the country, she took him to lectures on agriculture, so that he could learn about things he couldn't be taught in an East Side classroom. "She was one of those gals who realized that everybody had to go his own way," Jimmy recalls proudly.

He was about eleven years old the evening that she took him to hear a man talk about birds and the effect they were having on America's countryside. Young Jimmy, accustomed to breathing smoke and seeing girls at street corners going off with a dozen different men in a night, was transfixed. He heard the story of a peach orchard that was being driven to dust because it wasn't being husbanded properly, and to him that was a crime as bad as anything he saw on the streets. Then he heard about the tiny bird which daily ate several hundred times its own weight. Hearing those stories was more spellbinding to Jimmy Cagney than anything he could find in a Wild West tale. He wanted to find out more about the world of nature. His mother heard about the famous Farmingdale School of Agriculture in Long Island—so there, in his boyish handwriting, Jimmy wrote, requesting more information.

Jimmy hoped the school would send him some literature, which he could then take to bed to read or to school to show his teacher. He waited expectantly for the material to come. Instead, the school sent a man to the Cagney house to talk to the youngster who showed such an interest in agriculture.

The visitor probably had never seen so typical a New York family before, and yet as he opened his briefcase and gave the school's leaflets to eleven-year-old Jimmy, he saw his articles on farming and soil preservation being devoured. He must have left feeling even more puzzled than when he arrived, but he had done Jimmy a service and had helped win a strong supporter for what today would be called the ecology movement.

Just as Jimmy would visit his great-aunt on the farm, one of his friends used to visit an uncle in an insane asylum on Ward's Island. One day he took Jimmy along for a "treat." Cagney hasn't forgotten it to this day. "God almighty! What an education that day was!" For weeks, he couldn't get out of his mind the sound of people screaming inside this tomb for the living dead.

His elder brother, Harry, meanwhile, had decided at the age of twelve to be a doctor. Mrs. Cagney announced to the family that she thought it was a good idea and advised Harry how to study for his career.

At around the same time, the family moved to Ninety-sixth Street. The new block struck young Jimmy as much sadder than Seventy-ninth Street. There were geraniums on the fire escapes and black crepe hanging on the doors. Hardly a day went by, it seemed to him, without someone on the street either dying or being taken away in an ambulance. He was witnessing the beginning of what would grow to be an epidemic.

After changing homes, Jimmy also changed schools. He now commuted to and from Stuyvesant High on Fifteenth Street and First Avenue, where more was expected of him by his teachers—particularly Mr. Mankiewicz, the German instructor. Years later his son, Joseph L. Mankiewicz, was to become a famous Hollywood director and writer with credits including *All About Eve* and *Cleopatra*—but no Cagney films.

Jimmy liked his German lessons as much for the fun they gave him as for the chance of learning the formal German that Mr. Mankiewicz taught. In the class were a lot of Jewish boys and girls who spoke Yiddish at home, either because it was the only language their parents understood or because they themselves had come over from the old country. These children were finding out for the first time how similar their native tongue was to German, sometimes with humorous results. When a German phrase came up that no decent Yiddish-speaking individual would dare to utter, the whole class dissolved in laughter. Soon Jimmy, whose ancestors had come from County Leitrim not that long ago, was speaking Yiddish with the best of them, and enjoying every moment. He also learned German, but he spoke Deutsch with a Yiddish accent.

For the Cagney family, there was an ever-pressing problem of putting groceries on the table. At the age of fourteen, Jimmy took a job as a copy boy on the New York *Sun.* When he heard there was more money in wrapping parcels at Wanamaker's department store, he went there. He also worked nights as a bouncer at a local pool hall. During one period, he would get home from school soon after two o'clock in the afternoon, sit at the family table to do his homework, and steal a catnap. Then he was off to the Friars Club, where he worked until 3 A.M. as a bellhop. This was his first connection with the world of show business, but at the time he was concerned more with helping to feed the family, and being back at school at eight in the morning.

School holidays were times for more work. He'd wrap parcels at Wanamaker's in the morning and be in the pool hall at night, either bouncing or operating the switchboard. Sunday was his day off, and he spent it selling excursion tickets for the Hudson River Day Line tours.

Years later, Cagney was to say: "I feel sorry for the kid who has too cushy a time of it. Suddenly, he has to come face to face with the realities of life without any Papa or Mama to do his thinking for him."

Jimmy was never able to rely on his Papa or Mama to do his thinking for him, but his upbringing certainly encouraged him to look after himself. His mother gave him and the other boys boxing lessons—after her husband, a good boxer, had given her a few tips. At fourteen, Jimmy was his neighborhood's bantamweight champion. In those days in Yorkville, a fourteen-year-old couldn't go far without hearing the cry: "Hey, you! Wanna fight?"

For Jimmy Cagney, the answer always had to be: "Sure."

2 ANGELS WITH DIRTY FACES

JIMMY was developing both his muscles and his mind. Sharpest of all his mental attributes was that innate sense of observation, his ability to store away minute details. He could hear people talk and repeat their words and mannerisms years afterward.

He never forgot one classmate who repeated every sentence he spoke. He would say: "I was walkin' down the street today, walkin' down the street. Met this friend of mine, met this friend of mine...."

He remembered, too, the youth who wouldn't merely ask his friends how they were feeling, but would stab them with the greeting: "What da ya hear? What da ya say?" What Jimmy heard, before long he'd say, either in Yorkville or on a Hollywood sound stage.

Stuyvesant High School was full of characters. Some ended up on the wrong side of the law; others went to the tops of a hundred different professions. The school was very concerned about the sort of life its students would one day lead, and each youngster was asked to list his ideal future occupations in order of preference. Jimmy wrote first: "Big-league baseball player" and followed with: "Boxer, farmer, doctor, go to sea, drive a harness horse and be a philanthropist."

But this was all pie in the sky. For the moment, money was a pressing concern. Jimmy's father was constantly out of work, and the boys all had to take jobs to try to raise a dollar here, a few cents there.

Jimmy joined the staff of the New York Public Library as a part-time custodian. For twelve and a half cents an hour, he picked up the books lying about on the tables and wheeled them over to the shelves, where he then had to stack them. When he heard that with tips he could make more money working in a restaurant on 144th Street, he promptly gave notice to the library and got a job in the restaurant. He was doing so well there that he persuaded the three other Cagney boys to join him waiting on the tables.

When the restaurant's cashier was taken ill, Jimmy announced to the proprietor that he had the solution: a kind, scrupulously honest woman of Irish-Norwegian extraction who had considerable experience behind a till. Jimmy had no sooner promised to present this lady for the proprietor's inspection than a commotion was heard coming from one of the tables. There fourteen-year-old William Cagney—now known as Bill to the rest of the family—was having trouble with a woman diner to whom Bill had just served a piece of rhubarb pie. The woman insisted she had ordered a dish of ice cream, and was very angry about the mistake. Minutes later she stormed out, leaving a dollar bill and her powder puff. When Bill chased after her, trying to give her her powder puff back, almost everyone else in the building dissolved in laughter.

The restaurant was pleased to see her go. "What's your name?" he asked his young waiter.

"Cagney," Bill replied.

"And yours?" he asked Jimmy.

"Cagney."

Harry and Edward were asked the same question and gave the same answer.

"And who was it you were recommending to take over as my cashier?" the man asked Jimmy.

"My mother," Cagney replied.

Carrie didn't get the job, and the boys were fired for their cheek. Jimmy tried being a stock exchange runner, but he didn't get on with his boss, so he went back to tying bundles at Wanamaker's.

Harry meanwhile had signed up for a public speaking course at the Lenox Hill Settlement House, one of several buildings set up in turn-of-the-century New York to help make immigrants into citizens. Taking the course was Mrs. Cagney's idea. She thought Harry needed to be more self-assured before he could develop a perfect bedside manner, and learning how to speak in public sounded like a good way to help him.

Public speaking led to amateur dramatics, and Harry was offered a part in the settlement house's Chinese pantomime. Harry persuaded his artistic-leaning brother Jimmy to join the company as a scenery painter. Jimmy liked the people in the dramatics group, and got more and more involved in their activities. A few days before the pantomime's opening, Harry was taken ill and Jimmy was persuaded to take his place and make his show business debut on the stage at Lenox Hill. He did well enough to be invited back into other shows, including a play in verse called *The Fawn,* in which he appeared with his hair in ringlets and with nothing between him and his audience but a goatskin loincloth. None of his imitators have yet been known to recite the lines he spoke in that production: "Spring is running through the fields chased by the wynd ... the wayward wynd ran its fingers through the pinetree's hair."

That wasn't the sort of language used on the streets of Yorkville, and Jimmy must have been dubious about the reactions of his buddies to that performance. His consolation was the fact that his old friends were most unlikely to have gone to see it.

During his last year at high school, Jimmy thought again about his first and most cherished ambition: to become a farmer. An application went off to the Farmingdale School of Agriculture, the very institution that had fascinated him years before, but it wasn't able to take him for a year or so. When he left school, he worked for a time in an architect's office, but his mother decided that if he was going to be a good architect—and no son of hers could be any other kind—he would have to know more about the way the great practitioners in the field had thought. So, at Carrie's suggestion, he enrolled for a fine arts course at Columbia University, where his brother Harry was already a medical student.

Jimmy didn't get involved in fraternities or much social life there, and after six months he had to leave. In 1918, at the tail end of World War I, he was drafted into the Army. He planned to go back to college when the war was over, and stay at least until he could get in at Farmingdale. But when the Armistice was signed and Jimmy was out of uniform, there were troubles at home.

Both of his parents were frequently in the hospital—now his mother with gall bladder trouble, his father with a more self-inflicted illness. When the ambulance called to take him to the hospital, it was usually in an attempt to repair some of the damage caused by his drinking. Finally, he was a victim of an entirely different infection. The worst influenza epidemic on record was claiming people on both sides of the Atlantic. James Francis Cagney, Sr., died in late 1918. He was forty-two.

The younger James Cagney decided that it was his duty to

earn enough to feed the family. He didn't expect Harry to give up his studies at medical school nor did he want Edward to pack up his books. Ed had already been persuaded by Harry to follow in his footsteps, and they had plans for a joint "medical business" one day.

All four brothers—including Bill, who was still in high school—were expected to work in the evenings, but Jimmy knew it was up to him to keep a full-time job. Times were more difficult than ever; married men were earning $18 a week or less. Jimmy was lucky to be offered $16 back at Wanamaker's for tying parcels.

There was another reason why he and the other boys had to try for the biggest wages they could get: their mother was pregnant. Neighbors "tut-tutted" when they heard the news. Carrie actually overheard one woman tell another: "My, having a baby now! And her eldest already twenty years old!"

Their mother was the first to recognize, however, that even in the toughest times her boys had to keep up their outside interests. Jimmy carried on with the amateur dramatics at the Lenox Hill Settlement House. When the all-woman Hunter College needed a leading man for their production of Lord Dunsany's one-act play *The Lost Silk Hat,* they went to the settlement house in search of talent and chose Jimmy. He seemed to like his first experience heading a cast. In *The Two Orphans,* he played the part of Picard, the butler. And he was introduced to musical comedy there, too. He played the Emperor in the Japanese set show *What for Why.* When the settlement house put on an Italian harlequinade, Jimmy was Pagliacco.

But he didn't forsake muscle power for the more genteel arts of the stage. All the time he was also in training, and before long he became runner-up for the New York State lightweight championship. Still, the best fights, as always, were those out of the ring. And these seemed to come no better than the scraps at the Lyceum on the corner of Lexington Avenue and Eighty-sixth Street. When they were just scraps, most people seemed happy. But they frequently turned into riots. Jimmy tried his best to steer clear of those. He went to the Lyceum principally to dance the Peabody, a step he took up with some passion.

His favorite diversion was baseball. He never did take it up professionally as he had said he planned to do in his high school questionnaire, but he did become principal catcher for the Original Nut Club, Yorkville's neighborhood team. In 1919, the Original Nuts were considered so good that they were invited to take part in exhibition games. One of these was at the infamous Sing Sing prison in Ossining, New York.

It didn't take long for Jimmy to realize that at least five of his former schoolmates were now inmates at Sing Sing, and that day they all made their presence felt. They weren't officially allowed to talk to the players, but he recognized each of them as they called out from the sidelines where they watched the game under guard. "Hey, you, Cagney," one of them shouted. "Gettin' stuck-up?" Later on, he discovered that there were also at least two other ex-Yorkvillians in the prison hospital—and every other member of the Original Nuts seemed to know someone doing a stretch there, too.

The Sing Sing trip was to stick in Jimmy's memory in much the same way as his boyhood visit to the insane asylum. But playing baseball was just an occasional luxury for him. Jimmy had to think about feeding a new mouth in the family. His mother had now given birth to her first daughter, whom she called Jeanne.

Jimmy felt that the responsibilities he now faced were too much for a man earning the wages of a packer at Wanamaker's. When he talked over the problem with a fellow employee there, he discovered that the other young man had what he liked to call "connections in vaudeville." Keith's Eighty-sixth Street Theater, he said, was looking for dancers for a new production. Cagney had no great desire to become involved in vaudeville shows, but something his friend said made the idea irresistible: the theater was paying $35 a week.

3 BOY MEETS GIRL

FORTUNATELY for Jimmy Cagney's reputation among his old pals, he didn't tell anyone he was auditioning at Keith's Eighty-sixth Street Theater—and when he discovered what he was trying to get into, he was glad. If it had been known around the block that he was in line for a female impersonator's role in a show called *Every Sailor,* he would have been "skull-dragged."

Every Sailor was a show that had done a big business entertaining the troops during the Great War. President Woodrow Wilson had seen it at a special White House performance, and now, in 1919, the general public was going to be able to see it, too. When the show had toured the camps, the cast had included six servicemen dressed as girls. Now those men were back in civilian life, and newcomers were required to take their place.

As far as Jimmy was concerned, the only temptation was the salary. After the $16 he had been making at Wanamaker's, $35 a week seemed a fortune. As he was to tell me himself: "I'd have jumped through hoops if I could bring in $35 a week for the family."

First there was the little matter of getting through the audition. The management was looking for actors who could sing and dance, and Jimmy had never done either professionally. Nor had he ever had lessons. He had contemplated the idea only a few months before, but they were $3 a shot and he thought he could put that sort of money to better use. Now he decided that if he was going to learn, it would have to be inside that theater.

Luckily, Jimmy was one of the last to be called on by the show's producer. One by one, dozens of other aspirants were asked the same questions: "Can you dance? Can you sing?" One by one, they all answered: "Sure I can." Most of them could, too—which was also fortunate for Jimmy. As they tried out, he watched exactly what they did; then, hoping no one was looking, he'd copy their steps as he waited his turn. When his turn came and he was asked the routine questions, he bravely answered: "Sure I can."

Years later, he admitted: "I didn't know the Highland Fling from the Sailor's Hornpipe, and I couldn't even sing 'Sweet Adeline,' but I needed the job." He got it.

For about eight weeks, Cagney was on stage in drag, singing and dancing to a fellow playing a sailor. There were falsies under his gown and he wore the customary wig, rouge, and lipstick. The dance was described at the time as risqué, but the sexual overtones were really fairly muted by today's standards. Jimmy never felt self-conscious while working in *Every Sailor*. It was very much part of an actor's job at a time when the theatrical trade papers were constantly advertising for men ready to portray "wenches."

When Carrie realized what her son was doing, she wasn't entirely sure she approved. But if Jimmy was determined to go through with it, she, for her part, was determined he would be the best song-and-dance man in the business. On opening night she and her other sons sat up front. When Jimmy appeared, she issued the order: "Applaud!" The family did, and most of the other people in the audience followed their lead.

Most importantly, he was learning a great deal. In the streets, he would swap dance steps with others in the company. Sometimes he managed to sneak into the theater balcony so that he could watch the other dancers on stage.

When *Every Sailor* folded, Jimmy tried for another song-and-dance part. The Longacre Theater on Broadway was auditioning a chorus for *Pitter Patter,* a show that had been newly adapted from a popular farce called *Caught in the Rain.* Again, the salary was $35 a week. He competed with fifty other applicants, but this time, when the producer asked if he could sing or dance, he replied, "Sure I can," with great confidence. Now he was a trouper with experience, and he got the job.

Soon after the 1920 opening of the show, Jimmy discovered that he would earn an extra $15 a week if he doubled as a dresser for the star, William Kent. To his mother, the $50 a week he brought home seemed a fortune. He also acted as Kent's understudy, but there is no record of his ever having gone on stage in the lead part. When the star left the show, no one ever considered offering Jimmy the role. But he was allowed to continue as understudy to Kent's successor, Ernest Truex, and for the same $15 a week he was his dresser, too. When the show went on tour, he also looked after the luggage.

Although he didn't achieve fame or make a real fortune, Jimmy did make friends in *Pitter Patter.* One of his closest was Allen Jenkins, with whom he shared a dressing-room mirror. In years to come, they would appear in a succession of films together. But at the Longacre Theater, they were just two boys in the chorus trying to find new ways of making a dollar and meeting girls. Jenkins mentioned he had gotten to know a couple of girls in the show and one of them, he figured, would be just right for Jimmy. Her name was Frances Willard Vernon, but no one called her that. It seems that her father had desperately wanted a son when she, his sixth daughter, was born. Since her middle name was Willard, he called her Billie. And it was as Billie Vernon that she appeared on the stage. Her friends called her simply Bill.

Jimmy didn't take Jenkins up on his suggestion. He didn't like the idea of going out with chorus girls, even ones as pretty as Billie. At the back of his mind was the fear that the ladies of the chorus always wanted the most expensive steaks and the best champagne. He himself usually got by with a hot dog and a glass of beer, or a sandwich.

It was, in fact, while they were both eating sandwiches between rehearsals that Jimmy and Bill finally got together. Later, a doorman at the theater saw them talking and asked Jimmy when he was taking the pretty chorus girl out to dinner. Jimmy sidled up to the man and, thinking he couldn't be heard, said he didn't have the money. "I'll pay," said Bill, and asked where he wanted to eat. Soon they were seeing each other before and after performances every day, as well as when they were on stage together. In 1922, after *Pitter Patter* closed, Jimmy and Bill were married.

They worked out very carefully what they were going to do after they left *Pitter Patter*. They were going to have their own vaudeville act, calling themselves Vernon and Nye—Bill keeping her maiden name, and Jimmy twisting around the last three letters of his surname. Their act was no world-shaker, but they got a few bookings. When they appeared together at a New York vaudeville house, Mrs. Cagney brought her three other sons to the show. Jimmy's brother Bill was less impressed than the other members of the family. Years later, he explained: "I used to swell up with pride when Jimmy came out to dance. The kid was a pretty fair hoofer. I'd look around and tell anyone who'd listen: 'Say, that's my brother. Good, ain't he?' But dancing would never satisfy him. I could always feel it coming. He'd edge down to the footlights and a baby spot would pour pink light on him. Then Jimmy would sing. Boy, I sunk down into my seat then, and I wanted to be out of the way when they started throwing things. It was awful."

Other people seemed to agree, and the newlyweds found making ends meet a constant problem. They used all the tricks show people knew to keep up appearances. They used their makeup in the smallest possible quantities, and there was never any waste. They lived in shabby hotel rooms with a single gas jet on which to cook and heat the iron they used for pressing all their own costumes. They washed their own handkerchiefs and dried them on the mirror in the room.

The Vernon and Nye act was called "Out of Town Papers," but no out-of-town paper thought they were particularly good. The act was a compilation of three or four routines on which they had been working since leaving *Pitter Patter*. Bill danced and sang, and Jimmy played a comedian in a trick suit and hat.

Sometimes, they each went their own way. For a short time Bill had a "sister" act with Wynne Gibson, who was before long to become a Paramount star, and Jimmy was a single. In Lew Field's *Ritz Girls,* in 1922, the two acts were on the same bill, and things seemed to be working out for them at last. But soon, once again, they were looking for new openings, either together or separately.

Jimmy appeared in an act called "Dot's My Boy," which had been written by Hugh Herbert. The act had been running for years with Herbert himself playing the lead role of a Jewish boy working in show business under an Irish name. Herbert felt he was getting too old for the part and handed it over to

Jimmy, who seemed to take to it quite well. But he didn't want to limit his career to a role of that kind and gave his notice. From there, he joined the Jaffe Troupe of actors under Ada Jaffe. Mrs. Jaffe's son Sam was to be known as a distinguished character actor. Jimmy didn't seem particularly happy with the troupe and it didn't last.

In 1924, for the first time since their marriage, Bill took Jimmy to meet her mother in Los Angeles. He also used the time on the Coast to introduce himself to the big Hollywood studios. But no one in those pretalkie days seemed even remotely interested in a five-foot-eight redheaded song-and-dance man called James Cagney, and he couldn't get work even as an extra. With a new partner, Henry Gribbon, Jimmy went to work at San Pedro, but there was no more luck for him in California's vaudeville than there had been in New York.

Having invested in an apartment, the Cagneys decided that if they couldn't get managements to buy their services, they would form their own management—but not in a theater. Jimmy placed an advertisement in a local newspaper announcing the opening of a new dancing school. Since he had never had a dancing lesson in his life, this move was what his neighbors in Yorkville would have dubbed the essence of chutzpah.

Jimmy and Bill hired a small rehearsal room and waited. Their first pupil turned out to be a large Scot, who was almost the last, too. The Scotsman said he wanted to learn the big show-biz specialty of buck dancing.

"Let's see what you can do," Jimmy told him. As the Scot obliged, Jimmy grew more and more crestfallen. After unwrapping a parcel and taking out a pair of worn dancing shoes, the student proceeded to give an exhibition of dancing that Jimmy envied.

"I can't teach you anything," said Cagney.

"I din'na' think you could," replied the Scot dejectedly. The man had been trying for weeks to get a stage job, but despite his dancing ability was having no more luck than Jimmy had himself. He had been told his appearance was against him—exactly what producers were saying to Cagney.

Jimmy and Bill went back to work together, and soon their act was playing so many small towns that they called it the Cagney Circuit. The big vaudeville empires were known as the "circuit," but the Cagneys never approached their sort of success. Once they managed to earn $40 between them in Waukegan, soon to be known as the home town of Jack Benny. There they worked at a movie theater that presented vaudeville on weekends.

Often there was no work at all. One week they arrived at a lonely provincial theater with just six cents and their train fare home. They had to draw a $5 advance from the theater management in order to get a meal before the show started. Otherwise they were afraid they might faint from hunger as soon as they got out onto the stage. At one point things got so black that they had to borrow money from Jimmy's youngest brother Bill, who had gone into an advertising agency and was showing quite a head for the business.

In 1925, Jimmy joined a girl called Thelma Parker and another man about his age called Rand in a new group, which they dubbed Parker, Rand, and Cagney. *Variety* wasn't impressed. "Two boys and a girl with a skit that gets nowhere," it reported. "It's a turn without a semblance of a punch. There are no laughs and the songs mean little. One of the boys (Cagney) can dance a bit, but that's all. Small time is its only chance. Trio gets $275 top."

When the three were getting $275 among them it really was the top. Usually, they got much less. The act was owned by a man named Max Tishman, who called it "The Try-Angle."

Jimmy never saw more than $75 of the $275 collected and asked for more. When he put in his request, Tishman fired him and got another boy.

Next both Cagneys tried to make a success as single turns. Bill found herself a job in a New York musical, and Jimmy went around the suburbs of Detroit and Chicago. Bill, still working as Billie Vernon, rehearsed her New York spot for seven weeks without pay. The show opened, and closed in three days. Jimmy wasn't having any better luck. In Chicago, his hotel room was so noisy that the only way he could get any sleep was by using earplugs. He slept so soundly one afternoon that he missed an entire matinee. He never used them again.

Soon afterward, he and Bill were together again in New York. When they had work, immediately after the show they would go back to whatever tiny hotel room served as home. They never craved the night life, even if they had the money to pay for an occasional visit to a club. If they were not working, they would try to go to the theater to see others perform. When they did, Jimmy's sense of observation was as acute as ever. For him a night at the theater was an essential lesson in his craft.

Among all the actors they saw in those days, one man struck Cagney as the perfect actor: Lowell Sherman. He was "one hell of an actor," Jimmy said. "He could make a straight man out of John Barrymore." It was in a play called *The Sign on the Door* that Sherman made his initial impact on Cagney. His "heavy" act was a big hit with his audiences. He could be murdered on stage—and then get up and take a bow.

Asked why Lowell Sherman was so brilliant, Jimmy would have no hesitation in answering: "Along the way, he dropped the goodies. Anything you can laugh at, you can't hate." This was to be Cagney's motto throughout his professional life.

Eventually, Jimmy managed to play a dramatic role in a sketch with actor Victor Kilian for a brief period. When Kilian left to take part in Eugene O'Neill's *Desire Under the Elms,* he urged Jimmy to audition for the juvenile lead in the same play. Jimmy tried, but failed to land the part. He was told his height wasn't right, and his red hair the wrong color.

He gave an audition for George M. Cohan, but the great song-and-dance man bluntly told Cagney that he didn't think he had much to offer in his line of business. A young agent called Max Arnaud, however, did have faith in Jimmy. He thought there might be something for him in a new Maxwell Anderson play called *Outside Looking In,* based on the best-selling autobiography of Jim Tully, *Beggars of Life.*

As Cagney joined the dozens of other aspiring actors in the producer's anteroom, Arnaud told him to sit on the radiator so that he wouldn't look so short when the producer cast his eye over the people waiting for him. As the minutes rolled by and the heat rising from the radiator got more intense, the smile Jimmy was told to keep on his face became drenched in sweat. His trousers were so hot they were beginning to scorch. But the ordeal paid off when the producer came into the waiting room.

"I want a fresh young mutt," he said. Looking in Cagney's direction, he added: "You're it."

4 FOOTLIGHT PARADE

THE CRITICS and the audience at the Greenwich Village Playhouse on September 8, 1925, were excited by Jimmy's performance as "Little Red"—which from time to time had been his own nickname. The star was Charles Bickford, who was soon to make a considerable name for himself in Hollywood. But the New York *Herald Tribune* found space to praise Cagney's performance, which they said was "complete." Three months after the Village opening, the play moved to the Thirty-ninth Street Theater on Broadway. Cagney was to stay there for the play's run of 113 performances.

Now he was being talked about wherever theater people gathered. Many could be heard at Sardi's discussing what critic Percy Hammond had said about him. Cagney, he wrote, made John Barrymore's Hamlet seem "a mere feat of elocution." Another critic said that Jimmy "made a ten-minute silence something that many a more established actor might watch with profit."

After the play's run, Jimmy hoped for another dramatic

role that would allow him to make an even bigger impact. It didn't come. Just as he appeared to be on the threshold of the really big break, he suffered his biggest disappointment to date.

He had been signed to play the lead role of Roy Lane in the London production of the new hit play *Broadway*. Lee Tracy was starring in the New York version, and Cagney was rehearsing the role in Manhattan while waiting for the time to sail to England. Their luggage was already in the ship's hold, and a farewell party for Jimmy and Bill was just about to start when the news arrived at the theater where he was rehearsing. The producer didn't think Jimmy was right for the role. Since he had been contracted to the play, Cagney would still get his money, but the best the management was prepared to offer was the chance to be Lee Tracy's understudy. With nothing else in view, Cagney accepted the offer. Eventually, he was also to take over the featured but subsidiary role of Mike when Roy R. Lloyd left the cast.

For a time, he toyed with the idea of giving up show business for good, but nothing else seemed to offer the money he needed not just to keep Bill and himself but to help his mother and sister, too. To him there was nothing magnetic about the smell of greasepaint. If someone had told him there would be $100 a week for life for him if he packed up and went to work on a farm, he certainly would have gone. Edward G. Robinson, by now doing very well for himself in the Broadway theater, invited Jimmy to join him in a Theater Guild production, but he turned it down. The Guild—one of the most prestigious repertory companies in America—didn't offer enough cash.

In September 1927, Jimmy was offered a supporting role in Daniel Rubin's play *Women Go On for Ever*. Because it was a chance to play a serious role in what he considered an important serious play, he took it. Alexander Woollcott obviously thought Cagney had made the right decision. He wrote in the *Morning World:* "It is played to the hilt by a good cast, wherein Mary Boland, as the raffish landlady, gives the best and the most temperate performance she has vouchsafed us in several unbridled seasons and wherein all the cast is good, notably I think, Osgood Perkins and James Cagney."

While *Women Go On for Ever* was playing at the Forest Theater, Cagney's own woman thought that she could go on working forever, too. Bill went back to the dancing school business with a new establishment at Elizabeth, New Jersey. She called it the Cagné School of Dancing—it seemed to have more class that way. But this school didn't show any more signs of success than had the one in California. It was the sound of Jimmy's dancing feet that were heard there more than anyone else's. The young couple had an abundance of bad debts.

Women Go On for Ever didn't go on beyond early 1928. After it closed, Jimmy went back to being a song-and-dance man in the Grand Street Follies, produced at the Booth Theater. The show was billed as a "Topical Revue of the Season" and included acts ranging from a skit on commercial radio to a party on board an ocean liner. At the foot of the program was the note: "Dances by James Cagney." Stephen Rathbun commented in the New York *Sun:* "Among the other features of the revue worth noting were a comical burlesque of talking pictures, the Spanish dancing of Sophia Delza and the American dancing of James Cagney."

When the 1928 Follies ended, it was replaced by the Grand Street Follies of 1929, with more songs and American dancing by James Cagney. He followed the fifty-three performances in the new version by seeking and finally landing a part in George Kelly's new play, *Maggie the Magnificent,* at the Cort Theater.

It was an important episode in the Cagney story. The girl playing opposite him was a dynamic youngster called Joan Blondell.

The two auditioned for their parts in the play at the same time. Joan sat in a room at the New York Bond Building wearing a brown beret and an embarrassed, nervous look on her face. Jimmy came into the room and winked at her. When Kelly called to "the young lady in the brown beret," Jimmy winked again. "You're going to get the part," he told her.

The next day at the Cort, she was formally introduced to the male lead—James Cagney. Years later, she was to say that she fell in love with him that very moment, only to be floored when Kelly invited the entire cast to lunch at the nearby English Tearoom, where *Mrs.* Cagney had reserved a booth. But Joan said when she saw the way Jimmy and Bill greeted each other, that was the last idea she had of any romantic attachment between them. It was, however, the beginning of a long friendship.

Brooks Atkinson liked the play. Writing in *The New York Times,* he paid tribute to the young man who was "played with clarity and spirit by James Cagney and the gum-chewing, posing, brazen jade played by Joan Blondell." In the *Evening Journal,* Jimmy himself reflected on his life on the stage: "You don't make money in this business. But it's a living. Maybe, the work isn't steadier than running a street car or taxicab, but I don't mind being an actor. Maybe, I'll never be a good one—but you never can tell in this business. One good part makes you."

After that prophetic statement, he made two others: "When I get tired of this life, I'd like to try the movies. I hear there's good money in that. By the way, little Joan Blondell ought to go places. These movie people are dumb if they don't grab her."

The box-office receipts didn't match the enthusiasm of the critics, and *Maggie the Magnificent* closed after a mere thirty-two performances. But not before William Keighley, then one of Broadway's most respected directors, had seen it. He invited both Cagney and Blondell to join the cast of his new play, *Penny Arcade* by Marie Baumer. That play didn't break any records, either. In fact, it ran for only twenty-four performances, but it was seen by people who realized there was something special going on behind the footlights. Others who had heard about the pair's performances in *Maggie the Magnificent* came to see them in the new play and were delighted.

Behind the scenery, in the wings, and in the narrow corridors leading to the dressing rooms, performers were buzzing about some of the names who were in the audience for opening night. One name that was whispered louder than the rest was that of Al Jolson, who had wrought an entertainment revolution when he starred in the first talkie, *The Jazz Singer.*

"Jolie," as all the show people knew him, was the biggest and brashest Broadway performer of all time, a man who called himself "the world's greatest entertainer" and never heard anyone contradict him. That opening night when the curtain finally came down, Jolson was the first to go backstage to congratulate the stars. His first call, however, was on Keighley—to offer to buy the show. When he came around to give Joan Blondell a friendly peck on the cheek and to pat Jimmy on the back, he already had the deal in his pocket.

The next day, Jolson was on the phone to California. "Listen," he ordered Darryl Zanuck, who was sitting in his office at the Warner Bros. Burbank studio, "I've just seen the best play on Broadway and I know something about that street. And, I'll tell yer, it'll make the swellest movie, too."

Zanuck didn't hesitate. The year before, with *The Singing*

Fool, Jolson had scored the biggest success in Hollywood's history—a record to remain intact until *Gone with the Wind* ten years later. More important, Jolson always knew what he was buying, and Zanuck was afraid that if he didn't buy the package someone else would—and they might even entice Jolson himself along with everything else. Just as he was about to succumb to Jolson's deal, the entertainer put forward a condition: "You've gotta have the two leads, too. They're the swellest couple of kids I've ever seen. A gal called Joan Blondell. The fella's . . . James Cagney."

To keep Jolson sweet, Zanuck agreed on a deal, but sent a scout to the Fulton Theater to see *Penny Arcade.* Jimmy heard about the man's visit but assumed he was just there to sign Joan Blondell. At the end of the show, the man from Warner's knocked on both their dressing-room doors and asked simply: "Would you like to come to Hollywood?"

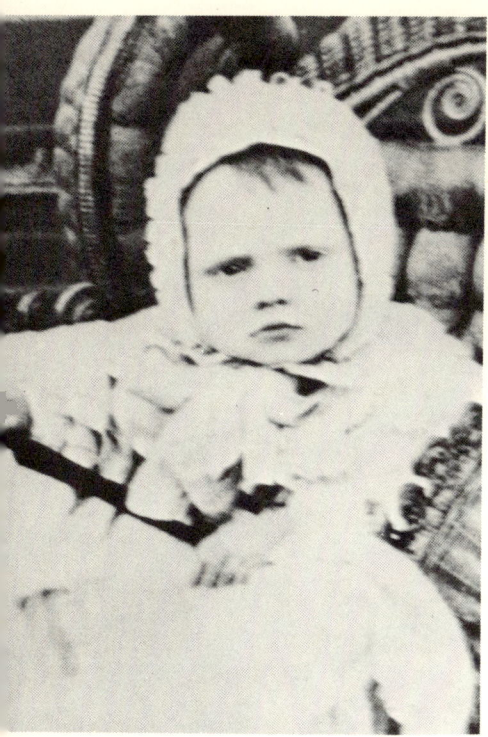

Left: Probably the first picture of James Cagney—age eight months.

Below: His first professional appearance as a "chorus girl" (third from left, standing) in *Every Sailor* at Keith's 86th Street Theater.

One of his first ambitions was to be a professional baseball player. The nearest he got to it was at eighteen as a catcher (second from left, standing) for the Original Nut Club of Yorkville.

With Joan Blondell in what was for both of them their first screen appearance, *Sinners' Holiday*.

With Edward G. Robinson in *Smart Money*.

The moment that started it all—the famous "Grapefruit Scene" from *The Public Enemy* (1931) with Mae Clarke at the receiving end.

With Loretta Young in *Taxi*. The Hays Office wanted more love and less war.

Above: Footlight Parade—and some of the mainstays of the Warner Brothers "stable"—Ruby Keeler, James Cagney, Joan Blondell, Frank McHugh and Dick Powell.
Below: A friendlier approach to Mae Clarke in *Lady Killer.*

Above: Classic James Cagney as the wronged convict in *Each Dawn I Die*—with Jane Bryan and George Bancroft.
Below Left: With his old friend, Allen Jenkins, in *St. Louis Kid.*
Below Right: Cagney the broadcaster with Al Jolson and Alice Faye.

Above: Cagney as Cohan with Joan Leslie in *Yankee Doodle Dandy*.
Right: "You're a grand old flag"—with his sister Jeanne, Joan Leslie, who played his wife, Walter Huston, his father, and Rosemary De Camp, his mother.

Above: The Roaring Twenties. *Below Left:* "What da ya hear? What da ya say?" with the Dead End Kids in *Angels with Dirty Faces*.
Below Right: Getting ready to punch his way through *City for Conquest;* on the extreme left is Frank McHugh, and on the extreme right George Tobias.

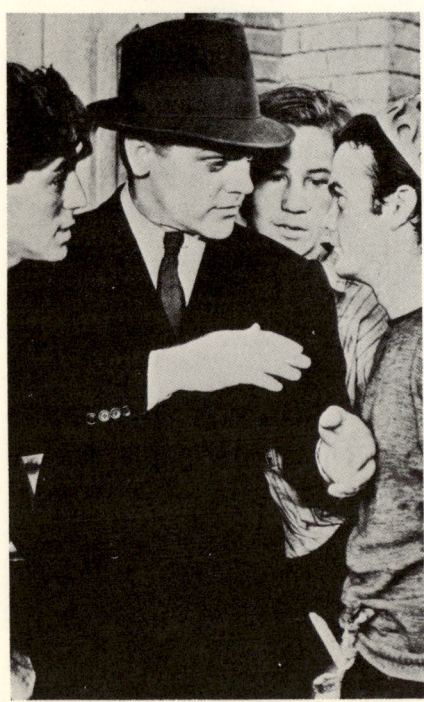 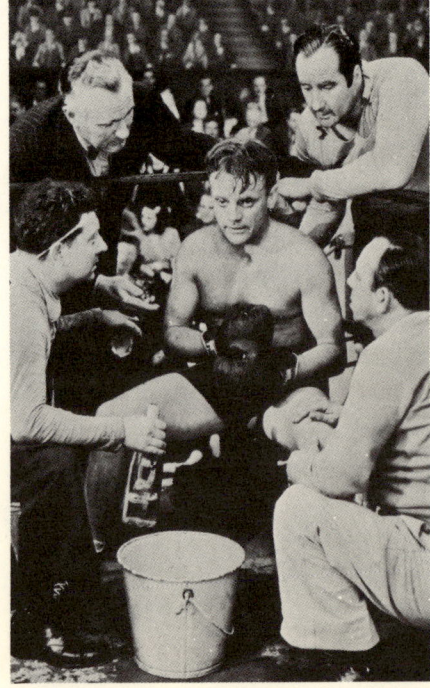

Above: Not yet "top of the world," with Margaret Wycherly as his Ma in *White Heat*.
Below: The end of a not-so-perfect flight with Bette Davis in *The Bride Came COD*.

Not the best Cagney musical this; with Virginia Mayo in *West Point Story* or, as it was known in Britain, *Fine and Dandy*.

With Doris Day in the film that won him an Oscar nomination, *Love Me or Leave Me*.

Next page: James Cagney at seventy-four. Recipient of the American Film Institute's Life Achievement Award, and Superstar.

5 PICTURE SNATCHER

IT WAS the dawn of the most exciting period in Hollywood's history. Sound had more than revolutionized the cinema; it was changing the entertainment habits of people on both sides of the Atlantic, and there were plenty of hoofers joining the soup lines. Vaudeville was already dying, and Cagney couldn't have gotten out at a better time.

Jimmy and Bill arrived in California not knowing what to expect. Neither Cagney nor Joan Blondell, who arrived with them, had a contract; that was still to be arranged with Zanuck. All they had been actually given was a couple of railroad tickets. Bill's mother still lived in Los Angeles, so they were not alone. But they didn't have any money to spend in the smart places of the movie town; and a lot of the excitement that was felt by other newcomers to Hollywood who went to places like the Montmartre for dinner on their first night out was missing.

When Cagney and Blondell went to the studio, they found that Warner Bros. was committing itself to very little. Both players were on the payroll for just three weeks—with Jimmy getting $450 a week—and with only the possibility of renewal after that. In cinema terms, they were both nobodies. Yet for years, Zanuck was to insist that it was Jimmy who made the first problem. He said that Cagney thought him much too young—he was still in his twenties—to be a Hollywood mogul and wouldn't negotiate. In the end, the Warner executive had to send an older man to set up the deal with his two "finds." To make matters worse for their initial relationship, when the contract was ready for signature and they went into his office for the first time, Zanuck was not sitting at his desk. Instead his seat was occupied by Rin Tin Tin.

Zanuck eventually arrived and told Jimmy and Joan what he had planned for them. He had been thinking about *Penny Arcade,* and he wanted some changes made. For one thing, he was changing the title to *Sinners' Holiday.* For another, he was giving them both different roles to play. Later, when he saw the results of the test they made, Zanuck decided that the Broadway director had been right. He reinstated both Cagney and Blondell in their old parts, and it was to prove to be a sensible decision.

Warner Bros. was happy with *Sinners' Holiday,* and well it might have been. The fifty-five-minute picture was completed in just the three weeks for which their two new artists were contracted. When it was over, both options were taken up.

Sinners' Holiday contained two ingredients that before long would be a basic part of a Cagney Warner Bros. film—a gun and a mother—with Prohibition and an attractive moll thrown in for good measure. The mother, played by a large shapeless Lucille La Verne, was the owner of the penny arcade which gave its name to the original play. Jimmy played her son Harry, who accidentally kills the liquor baron for whom he is working.

The film's dialogue was pure Hollywood hokum. Its effect

lay in the number of times Cagney's appeal to his mother was repeated in speeches like: "I didn't mean to, Ma. I couldn't help it. Honest I couldn't. Don't leave me. You've got to believe me. You've got to help me. I'm scared, Ma."

For a low-budget picture of its kind, *Sinners' Holiday* made an astonishing impact. *Time* magazine said of it: "It is less a picture of action than of character, made so by the skill of Lucille La Verne and James Cagney." In *The New York Times,* Mordaunt Hall was unequivocal: "The most impressive acting is done by James Cagney in the role of Harry Delano. His fretful tenseness during the closing scenes is conveyed with sincerity." Without realizing it, Hall was coining two phrases that were to become the Cagney trademark: "fretful tenseness" coupled with "sincerity."

It was the age of the gangster film, and Hollywood claimed that its duty was to reflect the world around it—a world in which gangsters drove the streets of New York and Chicago with machine guns next to their steering wheels. Right after *Sinners' Holiday* Jimmy made another gangster film, *Doorway to Hell.* It was the story of a bootlegging operation that Cagney takes over from Lew Ayres, who was very much the star of the piece. But a couple of critics thought Jimmy's characterization was worth noting. Warner Bros., meanwhile, was more interested in getting him to justify its investment of $450 a week by working in another picture. They chose *Other Men's Women,* a tough story about a group of railroad men and their marital tangles.

The Cagneys still weren't most people's idea of a Hollywood couple. They didn't spend their money at the smart restaurants, and Jimmy didn't drink enough to make bars a tempting proposition either. Because of the effect of drink on their father his brothers had actually taken the pledge. Jimmy didn't go that far; he said he just didn't enjoy more than an occasional glass of any alcoholic beverage, and never saw any point in drinking simply to be sociable.

Warner Bros., which had now made up its mind to keep Cagney on the payroll as long as possible, gave him a questionnaire to fill out. One of the questions was: "Why did you want to become a film actor?" His answer: "Needed the job." They also asked him his date of birth. When he wrote July 17, 1899, they changed the year to 1904—they didn't want the public to think of him as anything but a man of the twentieth century. Jimmy didn't like their thinking, but he realized that the professional thing was to go along with them.

In his fourth picture, Cagney played alongside a man he had been admiring from afar for years: George Arliss. It was to be the shortest role in Cagney's career, but his one scene in *The Millionaire,* in which he played an insurance salesman giving the incredibly rich Arliss the "spiel," was carefully studied by the Warner Bros. casting directors. He was on screen for no more than three or four minutes, but they were undoubtedly the most important segment in the film and perhaps, in retrospect, the most important three or four minutes in Cagney's whole career.

The scene took place in a garden. The brash young salesman, in his best pinstripe suit and white hat, talked to Arliss as he sat in a wheelchair. Arliss was one of Warner's biggest stars, a man who would play Disraeli and Rothschild and send women into hysterical swoons. But this scene was being stolen by a comparative newcomer. In it, Cagney was supposed to change the old man's whole perspective on life. He did it so convincingly that to the people in the audience the change in the millionaire's attitude seemed not just possible but inevitable. It was a triumph.

One reason Jimmy's performance was so convincing was that he took the advice offered by his director, John Adolfi.

"You look right for the part," said Adolfi. "But there *is* something wrong."

"What?" Jimmy asked.

"Your voice—raise it a bit. Make it sound more staccato."

Cagney raised his voice. His sentences came out more clipped, and another trademark was established without anyone's realizing it.

Cagney was plainly delighted with the result, but he was worried about the effects of upstaging a veteran like Arliss. The older man put his mind at rest by giving him some advice on how he could improve his acting still further.

Warner Bros. was the first to realize what that scene in *The Millionaire* achieved for Jimmy. They told him to report to the set where they were getting ready for a new picture. This time, it was to be a milestone more easily recognized as such. The title: *The Public Enemy*.

6 THE PUBLIC ENEMY

No one really expected *The Public Enemy* to be more than just another film about hoodlums from the studio that was specializing in that product. The script's main character was straight out of the Warner Bros. mold: a young man in a tuxedo with a gun in his hand. For Jimmy Cagney it looked like business as usual—earning his $450 a week as a cog in the studio machine. As he was to put it a few years later: "If someone blew a whistle and said 'act,' I acted." The difference was that, with this film, the studio realized the potential that Jimmy seemed to be offering. Gradually, they gave him the chance to build up his part and put the stamp of his own individuality on it.

The Public Enemy began to take shape when Warner Bros. bought a story called "Beer and Blood," written by two newspapermen, Kubec Glasmon and John Bright. Supposedly, it was based on the life of a Prohibition-era bootlegger called Tom Druggan. To the studio, it seemed a perfect follow-up to the record-breaking triumph they had just scored with *Little Caesar*.

The story revolved around two friends, Matt and Tom, who steal everything they can and then deliver the loot to the boss of their organization, a man known appropriately as "Putty Nose." Men are killed; a horse is shot; liquor is bootlegged. Warner Bros.' casting department decided that Cagney would play the secondary role of Matt. For the bigger role of Tom, they had hired Edward Woods, a dark-haired youngster who had two things going for him: he was very good-looking, and he was engaged to the daughter of Louella Parsons, the make-or-break Hollywood columnist.

Credit for making *The Public Enemy* the extraordinary film it was must go to Glasmon and Bright. They both had seen *Doorway to Hell*, and they both decided that Cagney was made to measure for their idea of Tom. Allowing him to play Matt would be an injustice.

The trouble was they could not get to the director, William Wellman, to tell him so. Wellman was so busy on the set that he would not see anyone. He was so concerned with getting everything right on the studio floor that for three days he didn't even see the rushes. The two writers managed to reach Wellman during the first weekend of shooting, just before he entered the projection room. When he emerged from his first viewing session, he concluded they were right. If Cagney did not play Tom, the studio would be the poorer.

The next man to be convinced was Darryl Zanuck. But Zanuck was not the last word on the matter. Zanuck was directly responsible to Jack L. Warner himself—and even if Jack Warner could be persuaded to agree, the same could not necessarily be said of his brother Harry. It was to Zanuck's credit that he made up his mind and decided that neither budget considerations nor the possible effect of the move on Louella Parsons should be allowed to interfere with the best interests of the studio. Cagney would play Tom.

It was obviously the right choice. Cagney was reacting to the story as though he were reliving scenes he had witnessed in his own youth. The dialogue was the kind he had heard all his life in New York. The violence that led up to the slaying of his pal and eventually to his own death in the picture was the sort he had often witnessed.

The picture was not without a message—indeed, it had both a prologue and an epilogue warning the public that crime never paid. When Jimmy himself is shot, he falls about the street clutching his stomach, murmuring "I ain't so tough." It was the most moving moment of its kind since Edward G. Robinson had died in *Little Caesar* whimpering: "Holy Mother of Mercy—is this the end of Rico?"

Watching the picture could be an unnerving experience. After a gangster friend is killed, Tom shoots his horse—to the consternation of animal lovers the world over—and later dies himself. Playing Tom in death, Cagney makes the most novel entrance in his entire career. His body, trussed up like an Egyptian mummy, is delivered by his killers to his mother's front door. When his brother answers the bell, he falls head first through the doorway like a cardboard cut-out of a man, blown over by the wind.

For years afterward, mothers all over America were to be horror-struck by the arrival of their sons in the exact same pose at their own front doors—among them, he was later to admit, a juvenile Frank Sinatra.

The violence looked very authentic. Real machine guns were used to demolish a wall; they were manned by a team of demolition workers who were to blow themselves up in a later movie. But the most real feature of all was James Cagney. When he did not like a man, he pulled no punches in saying so. "The dirty, yellow-bellied, no-good stool" became a classic line.

There was also a fair ration of sex in the film, principally in the shape of a young lady who could always be guaranteed to give any healthy man goosebumps. The original platinum blonde, Jean Harlow, only had to stretch her braless body across the screen to work her magic on the audiences of the early thirties. But Jean Harlow is not remembered as *the* girl from *The Public Enemy*. Nor is Joan Blondell, who again was being featured in a film with her old Broadway partner. The distinction, instead, goes to another blonde, Mae Clarke.

Mae Clarke was playing Cagney's mistress, aided by some singularly uninspiring dialogue. She sits at the breakfast table next to the disheveled, pajama-clad Cagney and asks him: "Maybe you've found someone you like better?"

It was Cagney's answer that caused the biggest cinema furor in a generation. He did not reply in mere words. Instead he grimaced, picked up a grapefruit from the plate in front of him, and pushed it squarely into Mae's face. In one short episode that movie buffs the world over now know as the Grapefruit Scene, Cagney had rewritten the code on the treatment of women on the screen. When audiences saw that scene for the first time, the shock wave could be felt across the continent.

Cagney said that the incident was notable because for the first time it showed a girl being treated as a broad. Although Darryl Zanuck later claimed credit for it, the idea was probably William Wellman's. He had heard of gangster Heni Weiss shoving an omelet into the face of his mistress and thought it would be worth working into the picture. Early scripts of *The Public Enemy*, in fact, called for an omelet, too. It became a grapefruit before filming could reach the messy stage. Wellman explained later that he got the idea when he felt the film needed some action—"and I didn't like the dame, anyway."

What is certain is that no one before had ever dared do

anything like it on the screen. Previously, unmarried women had either been in the gutter or were perpetual virgins. They were always thought to have hearts of gold and were usually treated as fragile enough to break. But Mae Clarke was being assaulted because Cagney did not like her. There were not even any sexual connotations. He was simply demonstrating that he was bored.

Critic Bosley Crowther was to call it "one of the cruellest, most startling acts ever committed on film." And Kenneth Tynan said Cagney in that one performance presented "for the first time, a hero who was callous and evil while being simultaneously equipped with charm, courage and a sense of fun."

Plenty of other people were misguided enough to believe that they, too, were equipped with that sense of fun. For years, Jimmy and Bill had only to go to a restaurant to be presented with trayloads of grapefruit halves. Girls even wrote letters begging Cagney to slap grapefruit into their faces.

On top of its other attributes, *The Public Enemy* was a financial bonanza for Warner Bros. It had cost them no more than $150,000, and at the box office it made more than a million.

The studio went out of its way to stress the positive aspects of *The Public Enemy*, saying it was part of Hollywood's war on crime and they hoped it would make women aware of the dangers of consorting with men in the underworld. But some people were not so convinced of the studio's missionary zeal. The New York police, for example, were not happy about the way they were being portrayed on the screen. Largely as a result of *The Public Enemy*, the Patrolmen's Benevolent Association unanimously passed a resolution calling for a ban on films that "glorify the lives of gangsters, gunmen, and racketeers." It was, they decided, a "very important subject concerning the welfare of the public." Representatives of civic organizations in Montclair, New Jersey, agreed. They met at the home of Mrs. William H. Taylor, chairwoman of the Better Films Committee of the city, and passed a similar resolution blaming the murder of a twelve-year-old local boy on the influence of the gangster film.

In England the film was called *Enemy of the Public,* and the British Board of Film Censors made it plain that was exactly what they considered the film to be. They banned it for a year, and when the green light was finally given, the grapefruit scene and almost every other violent part of the picture were shredded from the print. The scene in which the horse is shot was allowed, but the firing of the pistol was removed from the sound track. One critic wrote: "I have never understood the Britain censor board and I remain in the dark."

Critics all over the world were finding it difficult to agree with each other—sometimes in the same paper. In one review in *The New York Times,* Mordaunt Hall wrote: "It's just another gangster film at the Strand, weaker than most in its story, stronger than most in its acting." Another reviewer for the same paper was to call it "Not only a movie, not only a series of photographs on film. Not merely entertainment to be forgotten a block from the theater. A history within our history of a world within our world."

Yet another *New York Times* review described it as "quite a stirring gangster film. It is known as *The Public Enemy* and there is no glorifying of the thug. It is a serious study in the lives of two youngsters who grow up to be a menace to society." And the review added: "James Cagney, who had served on the stage for some time, gives a remarkable impersonation of Tom. It is as thorough as Edward G. Robinson's in *Little Caesar.*" But, as if cautioned by the patrolmen and the worthy citizens of Montclair, it added somberly: "Despite the undeniable earnestness of this film, one feels that it is high time that the producers scorned to put forth any more such tales."

If the public would scorn them, Cagney let it be known that he would be happy. "I'm sick of carrying guns and beating up women," he told reporters. "Movies should be entertaining, not bloodbaths." When he saw *The Public Enemy* again a few years later, he didn't like it at all. "I've never squirmed so much in my life," he said. "I sat there, my face burning, and watched myself hamming up the scenes."

Warner Bros. did not share Jimmy's concern with his "hamming." On the contrary, they decided to put him in a picture with their other current antihero, Edward G. Robinson, and have them play a pair of professional gamblers. The picture they made together was *Smart Money*, again written by Glasmon and Bright, whose standing with the studio had been vastly changed by the success of *The Public Enemy*.

Smart Money had a story without much depth, but it did live up to its title and earned far more than it had cost. Glasmon and Bright were told to devise a third vehicle for James Cagney. They did—and called it *Larceny Lane*. Once more Jimmy was playing opposite Joan Blondell, only now she had a better part than any she had previously been given. By the time the picture was released, it was called *Blonde Crazy*. This was Cagney's first comedy, and he played a hotel bellhop opposite Joan Blondell's chambermaid. Both seemed to be enjoying their parts. There were also women who enjoyed seeing Blondell apparently avenge her sex by constantly slapping Cagney. When she did it for the first time in the film, Jimmy told her: "I'd like to have you slap me like that every day."

Despite an occasional protest, Jimmy liked his work and the $450 a week it brought in. When his youngest brother Bill came to Hollywood he started thinking seriously about the financial aspects, only to shelve the matter for another time.

Bill had decided to give up his job in a magazine's advertising office—as well as his earlier ambition of a law career—and try his hand at acting. Jimmy offered him one piece of advice: "Never relax. If you relax, the audience relaxes. Always mean everything you say." When, before long, Bill signed a contract with United Artists and made pictures like *Ace of Aces* and *Lost in the Stratosphere*, it was plain he was not up to his brother's standard, and he knew it. He used to beg Jimmy not to see him at work. But where he *was* much better than Jimmy was in his business acumen. He boasted that he had not been broke since he was seven years old, and by all accounts, he had not. When he began settling down to life in Hollywood, he told Jimmy he should start thinking about getting a better deal for himself with Warner Bros.

Jimmy still felt he was learning his craft; and although he would never admit it, he was probably enjoying the notices now appearing with considerable regularity in the newspapers. The New York *World Telegram* said he was a "rising young talking picture actor to keep an eye on." In England, the *Sunday Express* said he had a "natural talent for talkie acting." And then it added: "Technically, his work is as good as James Dunn's—but I doubt if he will become so popular, because his personality is less attractive." So much for the perception of an anonymous film critic, and alas for poor James Dunn.

Warner Bros., impressed by the public reaction to their new star, announced that they were going to do big things for him. They were not going to allow Cagney to waste his talents playing opposite Barbara Stanwyck in a film previously earmarked for him called *Night Nurse*. Instead, they were borrowing a youngster called Clark Gable from MGM to play the part.

Cagney, they said, would star in a more important film called *Run for Cover.*

It was then that Jimmy decided he had finally had enough of working for Warner Bros. on their terms. He would make *Run for Cover,* he told Jack Warner, but only if he was paid more. If Warner would not pay, he would not work. The studio brandished its contract and said it would not pay a cent more than the document said it should pay. "Mr. Cagney," the studio announced, "will be going back to work." Mr. Cagney, however, said he would not.

Such a thing had never happened in Hollywood before, and no one knew what to expect next. Jimmy pointed out that other stars with his box-office appeal were being paid ten times as much as he had ever received, and so he was packing up. He and his wife Bill were going back east and he was going to become a painter. Ideally, he would have liked to pass up show business altogether and buy a farm. But he could not do that on $450 a week. So he and Bill took a train to New York.

As soon as he stepped off the train at Grand Central Station, he realized the sort of impact he had made on the screen. "Hi, Jim," called the taxi drivers and newspaper sellers. He knew he was a celebrity. But he was an unusual kind of star. When he left the station, he and Bill took the subway to his mother's house.

His familiarity to the public was not always an adventure. One day, walking down Broadway, he was spotted by a boy of about ten. Just as Jimmy was about to give the boy a friendly smile, the youngster said: "So you're the strong, tough guy, eh?" Before Jimmy could reply, the boy punched him in the stomach. He was ill for a week.

Warner Bros., meanwhile, was also feeling ill. They had a public clamoring for new Cagney films and a contract that said Cagney had to provide them. But no efforts on their part seemed to persuade him to relax his stand. He said he wanted more money because he had his future to think about. And, as far as the movies were concerned, he did not think his future was likely to be very long. "Actors," he said, "come and go. Of course, there's an exception now and then, but you can't count on that. Two years more, and I'll be looking for a job on the stage again, maybe hoofing. What's the use of kidding myself?" For two months, Cagney used this argument. Finally, Warner Bros. made him an offer: if he came back to work, he could have $1000 a week. He went.

The first thing he was told when he reported for work at Burbank was to take some driving lessons. He had never bothered to learn to handle a car before. On $450 a week with a large family to keep, he was not sure he could afford it. Besides, he never liked the noise of traffic. Now he had no choice. The studio wanted to see him driving in his next film, *Taxi*.

At first *Taxi* looked like an exciting venture. It was about the war between a huge taxi operation and the small-time firm where Cagney worked. The moral implications of a business war like that intrigued him. However, when the final script was delivered, it hardly seemed to resemble the movie he had first discussed. The war between the taxi firms was being relegated to the background to make way for a rather slushy, conventional love story. When Jimmy protested, he was told that Will Hays had intervened and it had to be that way. The Hays Office, which had been set up to try to "clean up" Hollywood, had laid down a series of rules for the picture makers: Even married couples were not to be seen in bed together; kisses had to be short and sweet; and the bad guys always had to come to a sticky end. This unofficial film censor also thought that at a time when people were still talking about the business of America being business, warfare between two business outfits was not very nice.

At Jimmy's insistence, some of the old fire was restored to the story. He was also allowed to make his own contribution to the story line. That would be the only way, he maintained, that he could be sure people would leave the cinema feeling they had been given something to think about.

Cast opposite him was Loretta Young, one of the loveliest girls in Hollywood and then at the outset of a hugely successful career. In this picture, she had to tolerate Jimmy pushing, shoving, and slapping her, and generally making her feel more scared than at any previous time in her life. "I don't want to talk about it," she said after the experience. "I didn't like the way I was handled in the picture, although it wasn't Jimmy's fault. I suppose he's paid to be rough in pictures."

He was rough, but he was also graceful, bringing in, as he sparred with her, a chapter from his past. The script called for him to clip her around the ear. Instead, he formed his hand into a fist and pushed it toward the back of her head. As she ducked, he pulled it away. "If I thought you meant it . . . ," said James Francis Cagney, Jr., recalling the playful trick used by his father in Yorkville.

It was not the only place where Jimmy brought his past into the story. In another scene, Jimmy is involved with a Jewish fare having an argument with a policeman. He settles it in the same way he might have done on the East Side—by joining in and speaking in Yiddish. No script could have told him to do that. No script could have called on the others in the scene to look at him in quite the way they did. Jimmy had always found his knowledge of Yiddish an asset in New York and something to have fun with. Now, he was having fun publicly and for the benefit of the picture.

Taxi also gave Jimmy the chance to help an old friend. The script called for a dance contest, and the dance involved was that staple ingredient at the Lyceum on Lexington Avenue: the

Peabody. The trouble was that nobody in the studio at the time could do the Peabody the way Jimmy knew it had to be done. But he did know a guy who had come to Hollywood with hope of an acting career and who could dance the Peabody as well as it had ever been danced. Jimmy had known him in New York, and now he was pleased to give him the chance at a big break. The studio took Jimmy's advice and hired the unknown dancer. His name: George Raft. Thanks to Cagney, he was on the way to a gangster-film career of his own, and he later became one of the legends of Hollywood.

Jimmy was proving that the things he did best could never have been done on the silent screen. His New York voice, with just the occasional touch of Irish in it, was made for the talkies. His lack of matinee-idol good looks paid dividends because his films were about the less attractive people in America's big cities. As one critic put it about this time: "He was fortunate that his face lacked the weak and pretty regularity of most film juveniles." Certainly, Jimmy made it clear he wasn't going to put lifts on his shoes or dye his hair. The red-haired Cagney photographed blonde in those precolor days, but if the studio didn't like it, they knew he would never do anything to appease them. So the matter was left alone.

Discussing *Taxi,* Forrest Clark wrote in the magazine *New Theater:* "James Cagney is the best young male actor in America, both in slapstick and the tragic genre, as well. But in his bewildering personality meet all the conflicting strands which make the films a delight and a perpetual torment.

"Cagney's most remarkable quality is his sterling emotional consistency. No matter how worthy are his fellow players and surroundings, he is incapable of false performances or of one foot of film which is not the candid record of his controlled impulses."

The London *Daily Express* commented: "What you have to

admit is that Cagney is an actor of great power whose devotion to his art never permits him to pull a punch." And then came this telling statement: "Although short and far from handsome, he seems to be destined for a long run in the stardom stakes. His acting is infused with lively actions that keep the cameras continually on the move." Such constant motion was very new in 1932, the year *Taxi* was made. As for the film itself, the *Express* said: "It is a rip-snorting action-packed talkie whose unpleasant, even sordid character may evoke annoyance, but not a tittle of boredom. If you have reached that stage when you can stand only one more racketeering picture, my advice is make it *Taxi*."

The New York *Daily News* made a prediction on behalf of a favorite son. "Cagney's popularity could equal or overrun Gable's this 1932. He has a grand sense of humor and he's one swell actor." To Cagney's delight and the Warner publicity department's credit, no one again thought of comparing the two actors in the press.

People were, however, thinking of Jimmy solely as Cagney the Gangster. One prominent mob leader told a reporter that he considered Cagney to be "the tops in my business." According to a story going the rounds at this time, New York's police department had a man permanently stationed in the balcony of the Strand Theater, which seemed to be showing nothing but Cagney pictures. When anyone in the theater cheered as Jimmy flattened an opponent, the police would nab him. More than once, the never-verified story goes, a gangster was flushed out of hiding in this way.

The Warner Bros. press notices did not help Jimmy combat his hoodlum image. He says today that he always took the "professional approach" in this regard and played along the studio line. But he winced when one Warner release described him as "Irish, but good-natured."

Jimmy was behind a steering wheel again in the picture that

followed *Taxi—The Crowd Roars*. It was about racing drivers, and again the screenplay was furnished by Glasmon and Bright. Again, Joan Blondell was his co-star; this time he marches her out of a room by the scruff of her neck, twists her arm, knocks her to the ground, and calls her a tramp. Every time he hurls an insult her way she tells him how much she loves him.

A London critic commented in the *Sunday Express* that British audiences would probably consider Cagney's performance to be "vulgar." But he added: "This is the sort of vulgarity on the screen that I am inclined to defend. There is nothing dirty about it and its excuse is that it portrays reality.

"Some of us in England are apt perhaps to be a little overharsh with films of this type. Characters such as Cagney portrays in this film do exist in America, and the existence of such extraordinary people is surely legitimate material for drama. My opinion is that Cagney is the finest young naturalistic actor yet produced by the talkies. I enjoy any scene in which he appears."

From racing driver in *The Crowd Roars,* Jimmy turned to prizefighting in *Winner Take All,* a part he made infinitely better than any script could have done, simply by once more injecting his own past into the dialogue. To play a boxer, he had to understand the thinking of the poor, nearly punch-drunk fighter who was sacrificing both his body and his mind for the benefit of a business organization. He remembered the way a once prominent boxer on the West Coast had almost lost his mind after a series of severe pummelings, and modeled his role on that man. But there was a more personal memory in it, too. When Jim Kane (Cagney) was asked where he had been before the fight, he replied: "I went out ... went out." The kid in Yorkville who repeated every sentence he spoke was being given a new life on film.

The fighting in *Winner Take All* owed itself no less to

Jimmy's past. The Yorkville bantamweight was more than able to look after himself in the ring. He shadowboxed and punched a ball with the viciousness only a real boxer could muster. He also trained in the ring like a professional fighter. For three weeks he sparred with former bantamweight champion Harvey Perry and lost sixteen pounds in the process.

Even so, there were a couple of tips a boxer "fighting" on the screen for the first time had to learn. For one, his blows had to look as if they were hitting without actually touching his opponent. He was advised to concentrate on the short, quick jab. He did so to an extent his instructor never envisioned. Jimmy's jabs were so quick that the cameraman constantly missed them. So he added a few round-arm blows, too. There was no dubbing in those early talkie days, so Cagney had to be sure he made all the right noises with every punch. He did, and the microphones picked up every sniff, every sound of leather against leather. Out of the ring, he made his fighter walk like a boxer and even kiss in the way he imagined a boxer would kiss.

Warner Bros. declared that the picture "fits his personality perfectly." As usual, they were right. *Winner Take All* made the almost statutory million dollars for them. When the studio head office proudly boasted about the box-office take, Jimmy announced that he was not as happy as they were, even though they had paid him $1600 a week during the making of the film. He still thought Warner Bros. was the winner and really was taking all. He wanted more.

Jimmy went directly to Jack Warner, who told him he was not interested in amending the contract again. Warner told his executives the same thing. On one occasion, he did it in Jimmy's presence, although he had no idea that Jimmy understood what he was saying. He and the other company men were talking in Yiddish.

Cagney turned his head—and then Warner realized why.

"Shtegan," he called to his assistants. *"Shtegan. Der Goy vehrshtayt Yiddish."* ("Quiet. The gentile understands Yiddish.") Jimmy's own Yiddish was so perfect that he sometimes felt like anything but a goy in that sort of company. What he now told the studio bosses was clear in any language. The $1000 he was officially getting each week was no longer enough. And he was not going to work any more until they paid him more. There would be no more films, no personal appearances. He was not even going to attend the premiere of *The Crowd Roars.*

Jack Warner had a new name for Cagney. He did not call him "goy" in public. He did not even call him *The Public Enemy,* although that was how he felt about his star. Instead, he said Cagney was "the Professional Againster."

7 HARD TO HANDLE

THE DAY Cagney walked out the second time, the Bros. Warner made it clear that they regarded his action as a declaration of war. Not so much a war between a successful star and their own operation, but a war between a fairly new figure on the Hollywood scene and the System. And to some in the film business, the System was not just the way you made films but also the way you ate, dressed, and went to bed. It was the Hollywood Bible, and Warner Bros. felt he was trying to commit blasphemy.

No words of caution would make Jimmy reconsider. No soft soap from anyone could persuade Jack Warner to part with an extra hundred dollars or two. Above all, Cagney was a pragmatist and now, in 1932, he was determined to get what he could while he could. He still refused to believe that a sizable number of people would even remember his name five years hence. So Jimmy and Bill locked the door of their Beverly Hills home and pointed their new car toward New

York. "I'm quittin'," he said as he left. "I'm through with movies for good."

One reporter asked him what he was going to do. "I'm going to be a backwoods painter," he replied. And then he had a second thought: he was going to study medicine. Hopefully, one day he would become a surgeon and might even join his brothers' New York "firm." Harry and Ed had developed a fairly successful medical office for themselves, and Jimmy was sure they would welcome him. Indeed, they had told him that some prospective patients were avoiding them for fear of being tainted with their "gangster" brother. Now Jimmy was making it clear that there would be no more cause for worry on that score.

Actually, Cagney had no intention whatever of joining them or anyone else in the medical profession. But he recognized that threatening to do so was a useful device to make Warner Bros. worry, and the studio's publicity department believed it. They made an immediate announcement that they expected Jimmy to become a medical student and that, consequently, he was now suspended. Jack Warner declared: "We are going to find out whether people who work for us are employees or whether they do as they please."

Hollywood had reason to worry about this rebellion, for Jimmy was not the only one playing it difficult. About the same time, Marlene Dietrich and her director-mentor Josef von Sternberg announced that because they had not been able to come to an acceptable agreement with Paramount, they too were packing their bags.

Warner Bros. had no idea what Cagney was going to do. He was alternating his promise of going in for medicine with the threat that he might do a vaudeville tour in Europe. That made Jack Warner worry even more. What if some European vaudeville group would pay Cagney the money he was demanding at Burbank? The chances of that's happening were remote, but he worried just the same.

On his part, Jimmy was still not budging. He said he was being exploited and had finally woken up to the fact. His pictures, he declared, had made more money for Warner Bros. than those of any other star—except, perhaps, the current heartthrob Richard Barthelmess and the comic Joe E. Brown. He knew that no one could deny that he was bringing people back to the movies at a time when they were staying away in droves from other films. Somehow, he had a recipe for making people forget the Depression. But he sincerely believed he was being asked to make too many films in too short a time—and for too little money. If he did not take a stand now, soon it would be too late.

He said he needed longer periods in which to work on his films, so that he could develop a character in a way that would make it live for him. But he was determined to be reasonable, and so as a gesture of good will he made an offer to Warner: "Let me do three pictures for the next year without any salary at all. After that, we'll negotiate new terms."

The studio's reply was simply to suggest that Mr. Cagney look at his current contract and come back to work—"or else be on the shelf for good." They also announced they were planning big things for actor Lee Tracy, who would now play the lead in a picture called *Blessed Event*, which had been earmarked for Jimmy.

Cagney replied to that tactic by saying that a goodbye to Hollywood would be all right with him. "I don't care if I never act again," he said. "There seems to be a curious legend that an actor can care about nothing but acting." That was certainly something he had never believed about himself. And he went on: "If I never have to do another scene, it would also be all right with me. I have no trace of that hamlike theatrical yen to act all the time."

In fact, the only thing he said he would miss was the chance to use the studio gymnasium. He had put on seven pounds since he stopped working. Yet he saw other advantages to his position: no more would he be asked to work himself sick while filming, and afterward find he had absolutely nothing to do. He often said: "I live in horror of having nothing to do. When you are finished, you are put aside completely, with nothing to do but sit around and listen to your arteries harden."

Jimmy was indeed worried about the effect of his present life on his old age. He and Bill made up their minds on one vital priority for the future: as soon as they could raise the cash, they would buy a farm.

"Life is long," he said, "and applause is short." Some newspapers were already writing Jimmy off, career and all. "James Cagney, who rose like a meteor, has gone like a meteor, too," said one critic. Another, using a similar metaphor, described Cagney as "more like a comet than a star." While they contemplated his decline, Jimmy just shrugged his shoulders and practiced "hoofing" in the lounge of the apartment he had taken in New York City, as a phonograph turntable spun at seventy-eight revolutions per minute in the background. He had always enjoyed dancing neat little steps. Now he was seriously considering how useful this dance skill could be. The vaudeville stage did, after all, seem the most likely new refuge for him.

But things seemed to be starting to swing his way in Hollywood. Mary Pickford came to him with an offer of a starring role opposite herself. Unfortunately for him, it was quite obvious that his Warner contract wouldn't allow him to join the Pickford-Fairbanks-Chaplin United Artists setup. Nor was Jack Warner in any mood to consider "lending" him. Then came a series of other offers from unnamed studios—including one proposing that Jack Warner should sell the Cagney contract for $150,000. Warner turned that down, too. More than anything, however, he seemed perturbed that Jimmy was content to stay away for so long.

Warner was no happier when letters started arriving at the studio defending Cagney's stand and begging Warner Bros. to come to terms with it. Jack Warner sent for Cagney's agent, George Frank, who left him in no doubt that the star was staying out. Frank had with him a report of a conversation between Cagney and a newspaperman in which he had said: "I look around me and see what servitude to the lights has done for so many—nothing. Men who have given the best years of their lives and the full measure of their talents to entertaining the world—and have never been paid in proportion to what they contributed—are now flat broke and miserable."

The odds were still stacked high against him. Warner Bros. not only had the System behind them, they also had their own reputation and background. They were among the big five Hollywood studios who had earned a place in the industry by recognizing the full potential of the talkies.

Born in Russia, Jack, Harry, and Sam Warner had started off with their father in the nickelodeon business, after Warner, Sr., had made his first dollars repairing bicycles. They went to Hollywood at the time Adolph Zukor, Jesse Lasky, and Sam Goldwyn were beginning to make fortunes for themselves. At first, they didn't earn much, and by 1926 they were all but penniless. But they had faith in a process called Vitaphone, which synchronized sound with the images on the screen. In one last desperate gamble they put everything they had into it. The gamble paid off and is now part of Hollywood folklore. Al Jolson sang "Dirty Hands, Dirty Face," from the screen and people in the theater heard not just the song but a mouthful of instructions to the bandleader for his next number. It made Warner Bros. the most prosperous studio of them all. Now, as they saw it, James Cagney was questioning their right to that prosperity.

The situation, they argued, went beyond its effect on Hollywood. The world was still feeling shaken by the Wall Street crash. "Depression" was the word that seemed to crop up in almost every conversation—yet people *were* still lining up for the cinema almost as frequently as they did for their unemployment dole. It was their one luxury, the one escape they saw from the squalor around them. They would pay the price to see a movie when they couldn't afford anything else.

Some studios loudly publicized the fact that stars and executives were taking salary cuts in deference to the economic climate. But Jimmy and Bill could see all too clearly that other performers were still getting much more than they were for less work and a lot less fame. Hollywood was still a place where stars drove in open limousines to homes with swimming pools. Actresses and stars' wives went to premieres and felt insulted if men didn't drool as they walked down the red carpet to the theater. But this was not the Cagneys' way of life. As Jimmy once said, "I never saw anyone fall off the top of a bus just because Mrs. Cagney crossed the street."

Now Cagney was saying that Hollywood should not regard itself as a world apart. The studio should pay the going rate for the job; and if the rate was high by anyone else's standards, that was the fault of the System, and Warner Bros. should face the consequences. "I feel that I have given the best years of my life working for inadequate compensation," he said. To back his claim, he emphasized: "A player should be in a position to demand what he is worth so long as he is worth it. When his box-office value drops, his earnings should be lopped off accordingly." He agreed he had been lucky. "Luck gave me a break," was how he put it in one celebrated interview. "But I do not accept the studio code." He said he thought he was going to do that vaudeville tour in Europe, and "after my return to America, I'll write a book called *Luck, Honor, and Obey!*"

If it had not been for his family responsibilities, he said, he would long ago have given up show business. He was still not merely providing a home for Bill and himself, but was helping to keep his mother and fourteen-year-old sister Jeanne, too. Now he decided he was going to stick out for $4000 a week. The studio replied by saying they were going to sue for breach of contract. And if Cagney tried to work for another studio, they would sue them, too.

Jimmy decided to adopt legal tactics himself. His lawyer, Arthur Sherman, pointed out that an "essential clause" had been omitted from the contract with Warner Bros. Most agreements of the kind, he submitted, included a section that said a star could be fired without notice. Cagney's did not—so he could not be suspended without thirty days' notice.

For the moment, Jimmy was waiting for the studio to make the next move, while hinting that perhaps his future might be in Hollywood after all. He took Bill out for drives in their car; together they swam and played tennis. "I'm taking care of myself," he assured reporters. "I'm not doing anything that will prevent my keeping in fine condition for my work." If conditions of employment improved, he said, he would come back.

But Warner Bros. were faced with a new walkout by another star and were determined to stand firm. They had just heard that Ann Dvorak was staying in Germany until *her* lawyers had ironed out money and work troubles with Warner Bros. The studio called a meeting of the Motion Picture Producers Association. It assembled in due solemnity, presided over by the same Will Hays whom they all resented for curbing their rights to make films with sex, politics, and violence in them. The moguls debated the effects of Cagney's defection and passed a resolution declaring that no "striking" actor would ever be employed by a rival studio until he had made up his differences with his own employers. The word "employers" was being heavily stressed. The fact that hardly a single resolution of the

Producers Association had ever been adhered to did not diminish Warner Bros.' enthusiasm for the new one.

One critic wrote: "It is time for us cinema commentators to have a good laugh." Warner Bros., for their part, were far from laughing; they were busy searching for a way out. While Cagney stayed away, they were losing not just their most valuable property, but also far more money than they would have had to pay him had they agreed to his terms.

The resolution finally came with the help of the Academy of Motion Picture Arts and Sciences and Frank Capra, a young man who was already regarded as one of the great talents among Hollywood directors. The Academy appointed him their arbitrator in the row between producers and star, and invited both sides to sit around a table and talk. After hours of haggling between Jimmy, his agent, and his lawyer on the one hand, and Darryl Zanuck, Jack Warner, and their advisers on the other, a conclusion was reached. It was announced that there had been a "friendly settlement," with Jimmy making films for Warner Bros. for $3000 a week and a promise of regular increases up to the end of 1935.

When the meeting was over, Jack Warner said he was "happy" to have Cagney back. The Academy said it was "glad" it had helped bring a conclusion to the affair. And Jimmy said he was going to "beat the hell" out of himself while working on his new films.

He was not, however, giving up all ideas of studying. Though he let it be known he was no longer aiming to be a doctor, he said he would like to find time to enroll at the University of Southern California and study psychology and economics. First, however, he owed his time to Bill, and he was going to spend as much of it with her as possible. He liked people to see he was a one-woman man just as he liked to emphasize how wrong his tough-guy image was in real life.

Jimmy's fans wrote letters to Mrs. Cagney, saying they loved her husband on the screen but felt sorry for all she must have to suffer at home. They were convinced that her breakfast grapefruit always ended up perpendicular to her nose. One woman advised: "The best way to deal with a red-haired Irishman is to use a rolling pin."

At one time, Jimmy even had to tell a reporter: "No, I do not use the wife as a punching bag." The idea that such a reply was necessary infuriated and embarrassed him. But it was a large part of the aura of mystery that still clung to him. For despite the new arrangement with Warner Bros., he and Bill still did not appear much in public or go to a lot of parties. When he had to make an appearance at the studio's request, he would stay just long enough for a glass of champagne.

He did not like parties, because he did not drink. Nor did he feel at home with strange women. He tended to shy away from any woman he had not known for a long time. If there were parties that he did enjoy, they were the ones at his own house and at the homes of close friends like Frank McHugh and Joan Blondell. At these, they would eat home-cooked food, tell stories—usually not clean ones—and dance. They would drink hardly anything at all. When they had "danced each other to death," as Joan Blondell put it, they would all sit around and tell more jokes.

There were plenty of people who would have liked to make more out of evenings like that, but they never could. There were never any orgies at the Cagneys' house. If there had been, Jimmy and Bill would never have fitted in. As Cagney once said: "I'm like Hollywood itself. Not all that I look."

8 STARLIFT

WARNER BROS. found an ironic way of getting back at the difficult Mr. Cagney. They called his next film *Hard to Handle* —which was exactly what Jimmy had promised he would not be in the immediate future. In *Hard to Handle* Jimmy gave a performance that *Time* said was "wholly successful in the character part which he discovered and which, with eloquent repetition, he has made peculiarly his own." In Britain, the *Sunday Express* said that Cagney, running from the gangs he was supposed to be defrauding in *Hard to Handle,* was a "grand sight and more of an actor than one expects from the earlier films which he has made." His comeback, they pronounced, was "assured by this film."

It was around this time that doctors discovered Jimmy had neuritis in his hands, but there was no evidence of any interference in his performance. In addition, Jimmy demonstrated himself to be quite a comedian in *Hard to Handle*. He showed as much skill at getting people to hold their sides as he had shown at scaring them to the edge of their seats.

His co-stars, Mary Brian and Ruth Donnelly, contributed to the picture's success and so did Allen Jenkins. But it was Cagney, playing a promotions organizer, who caused all the excitement. He based his role of the promoter-press agent on a PR man he had once worked with. "He never thought of anything but publicity," recalled Jimmy. "Used to make our lives a real burden. You'd see him jump up with a new idea. Next thing you would know he was on the plane for San Francisco."

The very idea of getting on a plane was a novelty in the 1930's. Jimmy and Bill would certainly never think of doing it. They made a pact never to fly unless they were together. But whenever the idea came up, they would try to find reasons for traveling some other way. The train was always "handy" and "more comfortable," or else they fancied the long meandering drive through the countryside. Several years later, Jimmy said he realized that Bill had decided never to fly at all. The pact she had made with her husband pretty well ensured that neither of them would ever do so.

The next Cagney film, *Picture Snatcher,* was more in the old Cagney mold. He played a former convict who works for a sensational newspaper, literally snatching pictures. Again, Cagney brought to a screen performance his own knowledge of the people who moved in the underworld. Alan Rivkin's script called for the photographer Jimmy played to snap criminals he had known in his previous life. As Cagney watches a woman die in the electric chair, there is a miniature camera strapped to his ankle—just as in 1927 a New York *Daily News* cameraman had caught a picture of Ruth Snyder being electrocuted.

It was an exciting story for its time, with Jimmy's closest friend Ralph Bellamy, as the city editor, proving he could turn a supporting part into a memorable role. The female interest came from a pretty newcomer called Alice White. By now Cagney had a reputation for shocking audiences, and people went to see his movies to discover what he would do next. In this picture, when he punched Alice White in the face, one critic said he had to stifle a yawn. Most people were more affected by it. Miss White certainly was. For when the scene was filmed, she received a real punch in the face.

Jimmy had never actually harmed a woman before. His deftness of movement, along with his unusual grace for an actor playing a "heavy," usually managed to give every appearance of knocking the daylight out of his leading ladies without ever touching them. But Miss White had never worked with Cagney before and didn't know his methods. So when he aimed a right at her face, she ducked—right into the punch that he had so precisely planned to miss her.

"Of course, it wasn't his fault," she said afterward. "But that didn't stop it hurting. It hurt dreadfully." Unfortunately, her pain didn't show. She was so affected by the blow that she forgot director Lloyd Bacon's instructions and didn't make it look as if she were hurt at all! Bacon ordered the whole thing shot again, this time with Jimmy making doubly sure that he missed. It was after this experience that the New York *Herald Tribune* decided it would be a good idea to form a club of all the girls who had been slugged by Cagney.

Joan Blondell—who always said how much she liked working opposite Cagney, because he had the gift of catching his leading lady's eye without the audience's being aware of it—was quick to sympathize with Alice White. "It isn't Jimmy's fault that a girl needs insurance when she starts on a Cagney picture," she said. "If you trust him, you can't get hurt—much. You need nerves, but Jimmy is as steady as they come. Jimmy's a swell hitter."

Cagney himself wasn't sure how he felt about this aspect of "just doing the job." As a professional, he did what he thought was best for the film—and he was prepared to face facts. "The public like it," he said. "There is no question but that at the moment, there is considerable interest in seeing women knocked out at every turn. But, like everything else, the public will get tired of it."

For the moment, the public were not getting tired of it. The New York *Herald Tribune* decided that *Picture Snatcher* was Cagney's film "all the time, and it is his personality that puts much of it over." That personality was aided by the usual Cagney homework. For days, Jimmy sat in the city room of a Manhattan newspaper, watching the reporters and photographers go out on assignments. In the paper's darkroom, he studied the way pieces of wet paper gradually became photographs.

It must have been useful to have this firsthand experience of newspapers. In those days, a Hollywood executive could see a story in a newspaper one day and be ready to start filming a screenplay based on it a fortnight later. Lloyd Bacon, in particular, could shoot a complete screenplay in fifteen to eighteen days. "He did things so quickly," said Jimmy years later, "that I once accused him of taking bonuses." In 1940, Bacon broke his own record—in one day he shot forty-seven scenes for the Pat O'Brien film *Knute Rockne*.

The idea of breaking speed records in his filming had no appeal for Jimmy. Nor did he like statistics. He was unimpressed, for instance, when *Screenland* magazine reported that 90 per cent of the 2350 people who took part in a poll said they wanted to see Jimmy continue to fight his way through the movies. Much to Jimmy's distaste—he was trying to get Warner Bros.' agreement that he should be spared making public appearances—the first prize in an essay competition that went with the poll was a trip to Hollywood and a chance to be a guest of the Cagneys.

However, Jimmy was so busy at the time that he probably

could not spend very much time with the competition winner. From *Picture Snatcher* he was moved straight onto the set of another film. *The New York Times* agreed that *Mayor of Hell* was destined for success. "Warner Bros., who made *I Was a Fugitive from a Chain Gang*," the paper declared, "has produced its equal in *Mayor of Hell.*"

They said it was not "remotely among the best institutional dramas, but it has a splendid cast and a sheer vitality that raises it out of the morass of an incredibly bad scenario. There are superior performances by James Cagney."

This time, the "superior performances" were by a Cagney character with a social conscience, a mobster who uses his influence to be appointed head of a reform school. He is tough, and so earns the boys' respect. He was also able to persuade the public that there was something inherently wrong in a judicial system that condemned boys to a life in a reform school. For all the occasional triteness of its plot, the movie was a stinging indictment of the schools and the whole process of juvenile law.

More than 350 boys took part in the film, taking a vacation from school as they crowded into the classrooms built on the set. Cagney, of course, made his usual individualistic contribution. The script called for one of the boys to sketch a caricature of Cagney, but the boy could not draw and the studio could not find anyone else who could. So Jimmy dipped into his past again, called for a mirror, and drew himself, as though he were still back in his old classroom sketching in a schoolbook.

Despite the success of his work in *Mayor of Hell,* Cagney was now more worried than ever about the pictures he was being ordered to make. Today he protests that he was never embarrassed by the gangster image. But it was undoubtedly a monster that threatened to overtake him. "We have to gauge ourselves exactly when to quit and try to beat the public to it," he said in a series of interviews.

Once more Jack Warner's relationship with the "Professional Againster" was beginning to cool, but the studio wanted peace. Warner Bros. made an announcement it knew would please him: "Cagney's making a musical." The columnists did not know how to react to Jimmy's new role. The cinema public, who now considered James Cagney a staple part of their entertainment diet, were not sure either. What was he going to do with all those chorus girls? Slap them? Kick them? Or simply offer each a grapefruit?

Cagney had finally managed to convince Warner Bros. that when he went home in the evening, he really did turn on his phonograph and start hoofing. It was such a regular part of his life that when comparative strangers George Burns and Gracie Allen called on Bill and Jimmy, they were each handed a pair of dancing shoes with bells in the heels and invited to hoof, too.

The package now offered to Jim was *Footlight Parade,* made in the now familiar Warner Bros. all-talking, all-dancing, all-singing pattern. Director Busby Berkeley was there to look after the dance sequences, and Ruby Keeler and Dick Powell hugged and sang into each other's eyes. The film also featured Joan Blondell and their mutual pal, Frank McHugh.

Cagney played the director of a series of musical spectaculars hired by movie theaters as the live stage "appetizer" before the main feature. In the best show-biz tradition, the leading man is found drunk and Jimmy, the director, is called, but it seemed to happen frequently in films of that period. Cagney's success was that he made it appear to be the most natural thing in the world, and not a titter of disapproval was heard anywhere.

The only person who did raise an eyebrow at the prospect of Jimmy's doing a musical was his brother Bill. "I asked him the other day, 'Jimmy, tell the truth. Which would you rather do, be a motion-picture actor or sing better than you do?' He said, 'I'd rather sing!'" Bill shrugged, unable to comprehend why anyone should want to hear him do it.

To Bill's surprise, people did like Jimmy's singing and dancing. He crooned "Shanghai Lil" to Ruby Keeler so effortlessly that audiences might have thought he did nothing else on the screen but dress up in a sailor suit and hold a sloe-eyed beauty in a split skirt on his lap. *The New York Times* added to what was becoming a series of tributes to Jimmy by saying: "The stars that hang high over Shanghai lighting James Cagney's sultry search for Shanghai Lil also reveal one more side of his astonishing versatility." The nicest touch, though, came from *Variety,* which managed to locate Cagney's ex-agent Max Tishman and ask him what he now thought of the fellow he had fired from Parker, Rand and Cagney. Tishman replied simply that Jimmy could have his raise if he would agree to go back.

In his next picture, Cagney was battling with Mae Clarke again, but this time there was no grapefruit in sight. Instead, the script called on him to pull her along by the hair, caveman style. The movie was *Lady Killer,* the story of a cinema usher who becomes, in turn, a hoodlum and a bit player in films. It was to be the only time Cagney wore an Indian headdress and showed a red-painted bare torso in a film.

Jimmy the Gent, Cagney's next film, was described as featuring "the toughest of the Cagney roles." He must have seen it that way too, for the day he arrived on the set for the first time, he had shaved off most of the hair from the sides and back of his head. He explained to stunned director Michael Curtiz that he thought he would look more in character that way.

"It's a bit too tough for me," the critic of the London *Sunday Express* said, reviewing the film. But in fact it was a comedy about racketeers, and a surprisingly curvy Bette Davis as his co-star was enough to ease most viewers' anxieties. Mordaunt Hall in *The New York Times* said: *"Jimmy the Gent* is a swift-paced comedy in which he gives another of his vigorous, incisive portrayals." The film was billed with the tag line: "No more slugging dames. He knocks 'em cold—with culture."

Next Cagney moved on to *He Was Her Man,* the last of his seven pictures with Joan Blondell, who this time played the traditional prostitute with the heart of gold. It was a sentimental story, and one writer addressed himself to Cagney: "In a changing world, I thought I could rely on you to stay tough. What was the idea of turning this flick into a sobbie, anyway?"

He Was Her Man was a Cagney milestone, if only because in a review of this picture, the New York *Herald Tribune* was to make an interesting comparison: "More than any other actor, Mr. Cagney is the exponent of the school of acting of which George M. Cohan is the brilliant dean. Eschewing histrionic fireworks, he is adept at calculated understatement in which the slightest gesture, the slightest inflection of the voice is extremely significant. It is possible that you do not care for the disreputable and frequently vicious type of American citizenry he delineates, but you cannot quarrel with the manner in which he re-creates them." As for the film, the critic wrote: "It is James Cagney's gift to execute a characterization with such clarity and conviction that a poor plot becomes exciting and engaging."

Meanwhile, most people were less enthusiastic about Jim's brother Bill's films. United Artists had Bill doing the same sort of thing that Jimmy did, but he reacted without Jimmy's subtlety. When he punched men and slapped girls, there was little to it but brutality. When Jim again suggested he would like to see Bill at work, the studio again begged not to. Before long, Bill decided he might do better as an artists' agent.

Around about this time critic Lincoln Kirstein said: "James Cagney has an inspired sense of timing, an arrogant style, a pride in the control of his body and a conviction and lack of self-consciousness that is unique in the deserts of the American screen. No one expresses more clearly in terms of pictorial action the delights of violence, the overtones of a semiconscious sadism, the tendency toward destruction, toward anarchy which is the base of American sex appeal."

As a result of that unique brand of sex appeal, a generation of American youth walked around with what they believed to be Cagney mannerisms—throwing punches and pointing index fingers wildly as they talked. Some of them even treated their women the way they believed Jimmy treated his.

In *Here Comes the Navy* Jimmy had two blondes to play to—Dorothy Martin, who left the cast halfway through filming when she was taken ill, and her replacement, Gloria Stuart. The film's second lead was Pat O'Brien, who, as a petty officer in the picture, fights Cagney and steals his girl. Outside the studio, the two were close friends. The Legion of Decency had told Warner Bros. that women should be respected, so the punches were strictly for the boys in this picture.

Jimmy, however, always had his own standards of decency. As the end of a day's shooting drew close, Cagney would sidle up to O'Brien and, with a wink, suggest: "Say, Paddy, what say we blow a couple of scenes so that the extras can get some overtime?" Director Lloyd Bacon knew they were doing it, but was powerless to stop them. Cagney and O'Brien messed up more than a few scenes to give underpaid, overworked extras a few more dollars.

Soon, however, Cagney was to feel equally powerless when he learned that his name was being linked with rumors far removed from the usual Hollywood gossip.

9 SHAKE HANDS WITH THE DEVIL

It all happened very suddenly and in another town.

In a courtroom in Sacramento, detective Roy Kunz announced he had evidence linking "Cagney, the motion-picture actor," with the case he was helping to prosecute. Since Sacramento is the California state capital and Jimmy was in Hollywood, the court had jurisdiction to hear the evidence from Detective Kunz, a respected local policeman who was building a wide reputation. He was a member of what was more and more being called the "Red Squad."

His evidence shook Warner Bros., made the tongues of Hollywood wag, and took James Cagney by total surprise. Without warning, Detective Kunz said he would be producing letters showing that Cagney was implicated with Caroline Decker, secretary of the Cannery and Agricultural Workers Union, and sixteen others being indicted on charges of "criminal syndicalism" before the state Supreme Court. The defendants, he said, were Communists, and Cagney was a sympathizer.

When Kunz started reading the first letter sent to Caroline Decker, the chatter in the courtroom was so loud that the judge called for silence. It said: "I have Cagney's money again," and was signed "Ella." The signature began to clear the matter for Cagney, but made him all the more angry and even more surprised. "Ella" was Ella Winters, a journalist and wife of Lincoln Steffens, the well-known writer.

Steffens was the son of an extremely wealthy self-made businessman who had given him an education at European universities. Then, without warning, his father gave him a check for $100 with the advice that he had better "stay in New York and hustle." There would be no more money from where the $100 had come.

It was Steffens' investigative brand of journalism that Teddy Roosevelt had in mind when he coined the phrase "muckraking." Later, Steffens, believing that America could benefit from some form of Bolshevism, went to Moscow on a secret mission to see what the Communist government wanted in exchange for a détente.

Steffens had made people like Sinclair Lewis and Walter Lippmann his protégés. When Cagney met Steffens, there was an immediate sense of rapport between them. Ever since Jimmy was a child in Yorkville, he had admired people who were able to produce fine things. He had learned to draw because instinctively he wanted to create. His acting had taught him love of words and a sense of admiration for those whose words stirred the emotions. Steffens was at least thirty years older than Cagney, but his age did not hinder their friendship. Neither did the fact that he had Communist leanings seem to be any reason to stop visiting the Steffens home at Carmel.

Both Jimmy and Bill became friends of Steffens' English-born wife, who contributed to magazines under the name Ella Winters. One evening, they were together when Ella moved the

Cagneys tremendously. She had been reporting for a national magazine on a strike of cotton workers in the San Joaquin Valley. The misery she had witnessed was beyond belief, she said. With her own eyes she had seen a baby die of starvation. Jimmy was so affected by her story that he immediately offered whatever help he could give. He wrote her a check.

That was in 1933. Now in August 1934, the gift was being discussed in the Sacramento court. And it was being given a totally different interpretation, one that grew more and more sinister as the detective proceeded to read the rest of Ella's letter to Caroline Decker.

"Cagney was fine this time and is going to bring other stars up to talk to Stef about Communism," she said. "He wrote a piece for the Screen Actors Guild—which, as you know, is the employees' rebellion against the producers—even the employees getting $3500 a week."

If this had been a film and Cagney had been in the court scene, he would doubtless have jumped on a table and shouted: "It's all lies, lies, lies!" But this scene was all too real, and Jim was at home in Los Angeles, totally dumbfounded by what was later relayed to him by reporters who had been there.

Then the officer read another letter from Ella to Decker, again implicating Cagney. The letter said he had offered to provide Miss Decker with all the typewriter ribbons she needed; all she had to do was call at the house at Hillcrest Road. But, it suggested, "don't give it [the Beverly Hills address] to anyone else." It also said that Cagney would provide Miss Decker with bail if she were ever arrested.

At his home in Beverly Hills, Cagney finally did put his side of the story to reporters. He said he couldn't believe that Ella Winters could write the things she had. And if she had written them, "she had no right to do so." He agreed that he and

Steffens were friends and that he admired the writer and lecturer. But as for sharing his views, that was complete nonsense.

"I'm proud to call myself 100 per cent American," he declared, snapping his fingers as though discussing a new film with Warner Bros. "This old country has been pretty good to me. I started with nothing, worked hard, and today am very comfortable." No one could doubt he was telling the truth when he summed up his feelings about the America of 1934: "I believe that nowhere else is there the same golden opportunity for anyone willing to work hard as there is in America." Then he put the situation into what he considered to be its true perspective: "It certainly would be ridiculous for me to align myself with any Communistic, Socialistic, Nazi, White Shirts, Silver Shirts, or any other un-American movement—because I would be the first to suffer should these radical movements' agitators succeed."

Meanwhile, the fight went on in Sacramento. The district attorney, Neil McAllister, said he was determined to prove that Cagney was indeed a Communist. At home, Jimmy and Bill tried to comfort each other while other members of the family came to lend their support, too. Jimmy assured newspapermen: "I'll spend every dollar to make McAllister prove his charges, which are absolutely untrue. I deny most emphatically that I ever aided Communists or ever intended to."

Meanwhile, other names were brought into the arena of the Sacramento courtroom. And it was this very "cast list" that finally began to weaken the D.A.'s case. Lupe Velez, Dolores Del Rio, and Ramon Novarro were cited—all top box-office attractions, but also all Mexicans with obvious sympathy for their fellow countrymen's plight. Would these stars have any reason to take a purely humanitarian attitude on the issue? As for Jimmy Cagney, it would not be too difficult to show he had always been regarded as something of a soft touch. He was very concerned for the welfare of other people.

Outside the court, the D.A. said he would seek a Superior Court injunction restraining Cagney from advocating or giving financial aid to Communists and would take similar action against the Mexican stars—once an inquiry in Los Angeles had produced conclusive evidence that they had a "connection with radicalism."

When Jimmy heard this, he answered: "I'm against all -isms except Americanism. It appears to me that McAllister's actions are a bid for personal publicity at my expense."

Then Steffens himself joined in, saying it was perfectly true that Cagney had given money "to relieve misery in the San Joaquin cotton strike last year." But he added: "So did other people who gave food or clothing—or money for food and clothing—when they heard those conditions being described or saw them with their own eyes. That's all." Attempts to link Cagney with radicals, said Steffens, were "absurd."

Evidently, the people making the inquiries in Los Angeles thought so, too. Jimmy and the other stars were cleared of any complicity with a Communist organization. But the charges took a long time to die down and were to rear their heads again a few years later. It looked as if he was suffering from McCarthyism fifteen years before anyone else. But Warner Bros. would not have dared employ anyone they considered to be politically "unreliable," and Jimmy was still very much in business.

10 THE CROWD ROARS

ONE THING was clear: James Cagney's public couldn't wait to see him back on the screen. They were delighted that the Communist scare had proved to be nothing more than libel, and looked forward to once more seeing him fight the law with a gun in his hand and a girl at his side.

The papers were glad to see him vindicated, too. *The New York Times* cheered louder than most: "He was and continues to be so brilliantly right in his interpretation of a particular type of American male—a type that has been spawned in large numbers out of the slum districts of New York City and Chicago—that it is a natural thing to suppose that he is not acting at all. Mr. Cagney looks, walks, talks, acts, and apparently smells like whatever character he is called upon to interpret during his embattled career."

The *Times* compared him with George Raft, who once reported that the gangsters he continued to mix with could never understand why he always had to die in his films. Said the paper: "Unlike George Raft, who seems unable to escape from the monotonous reiteration of the type characterization which brought him to public attention, Mr. Cagney, within the rather limited range permitted him, brings each role brilliantly alive."

For years Cagney had been asked to endorse a dozen different products in advertising campaigns, and he always refused. But in July 1934 Tough Guy Cagney could be seen staring out from the pages of American newspapers and shouting: "There's nothing tough about my throat." His statement on behalf of Old Gold cigarettes went on: "If an actor plays a few two-fisted characters on the screen, some people get the idea that he's hard as nails all through. But that's not always true. Take my throat for instance. I have to watch it like every other movie actor who works in front of a mike." The copy was written by an advertising agency, but in its way it showed Cagney trying to escape his image, saying he was not tough all through. Still, Cagney was not comfortable about making money in this way, and three years later he refused to endorse another tobacco company's wares.

St. Louis Kid, his nineteenth film and the first to be released since the Steffens troubles, was notable in that this time he was at the receiving end of a woman's punches. Patricia Ellis threatens him with a knife, too, but apart from all that, it had the usual Cagney plot. He played a truck driver with a temper so quick that when a man is killed at the dairy where he works, he is wrongly accused of the murder. Jimmy was more impressed with the story line of this picture than he had been with many of his earlier films.

Devil Dogs of the Air was a much better picture, with Cagney and Pat O'Brien swapping the uniforms they had worn in *Here Comes the Navy* for the garb of the Marine Flying Corps. There were some magnificent aerial shots, and it was a box-office hit.

The film that followed *Devil Dogs* was not only a more important staging point in his career; it also contributed to the American vocabulary. Producer Louis F. Edelman thought of the idea of putting Cagney, for once, on the right side of the law in an FBI story. He worried, though, that the Bureau's initials would not sell many tickets. The suggested alternative, *Government Men,* would, he thought, look even worse on the marquees. Instead, he called the picture *G-Men,* and it concerned a carefully organized FBI campaign to be allowed to cross all state lines when chasing gangs. Cagney, playing one of the G-men, made even the excessive preaching it contained seem no more than part of a story of which, as always, he had taken full control.

Warner Bros. exploited the novelty of the situation—Cagney and the criminals on opposing sides—in every way they could. The newspaper advertisements and billboard posters shouted the switch. The only one who had any doubts about its public acceptance seemed to be Jimmy himself. "When I was assigned to it, there arose a question in my mind as to whether the public would accept that guy as the rough mug of the U.S. Department of Justice." Like certain other big stars, Cagney sometimes lapsed into talking about himself in the third person. The difference was that here he was doing it deliberately, and solely for effect. "That guy" was the man in his past, the one who had always been on the wrong side of the law.

But the force of the Cagney personality ensured "that guy's" success. He played a poor boy from the wrong side of the tracks who trains as a lawyer, thanks to the financial help of a gang boss who regrets his ways. He opens his own law office, but the only sign of activity is the fly skimming over the unopened law books. The most telling jury speech is the one he makes to a mirror at the beginning of the film—a fascinating production piece that would have made Portia feel proud.

The Cagney in *G-Men* had an almost angelic look—until a shadow on the glass door panel reveals not a possible first client but an old pal (played by Regis Toomey, another member of the Warner Bros. stable) who is already a member of the FBI. He tries to get Jimmy to join, but Jimmy does so only when the friend is shot down by the mob he was trying to bring to justice. From that moment on, a relentless Cagney takes on his dead friend's crusade right through to a shoot-out in a remote farmhouse. Along the way there is a romance with Ann Dvorak (who had made up her disagreements with Warner Bros., too) and another with Margaret Lindsay, who plays the sister of Jimmy's boss in the Bureau.

For 1935, it had everything a crime movie needed. The New York *Herald Tribune* said this of *G-Men:* "Cleaving with remarkable fidelity to the Government's war on organized crime, the work utilizes to the utmost the cinema's cunning devices for melodramatic effect." For the standards of the day, they were absolutely right. The film looks terribly dated today. The cutting of some of the scenic shots is slipshod; the romantic incidents are contrived. But Cagney's performance is as sharp and polished as though he had just seen the film locked away ready for its first showing.

The *Herald Tribune* wondered how J. Edgar Hoover would react to the film's concept of G-men: "The treatment, when it is not frankly melodramatic, is inclined to a sentimental romanticizing of the Department of Justice's work which probably does not hold with the routine involved." Mr. Hoover, Warner Bros. was pleased to learn, was very pleased indeed with the way some of the routine aspects of his men's lives were omitted. Nor was he known to be averse to having his agents described as G-men.

Probably the best part of the film from the audience's point of view was being able to watch the way Jimmy worked with his hands. He was making them tell a story, just as his neighbors in Yorkville had done when they had no more than a dozen words of a common language. He always used his hands in a way that was instantly recognizable. Any Cagney fan watching a close-up of those hands would know them if no other part of his body was visible. Cagney used them well because he understood the importance they could hold. "A little guy has got to be able to spread himself around," was the way he put it.

A lot of people would have liked to see him spread himself around a little more in public. But only those who managed to discover in advance the dining plans of Jimmy and his friends ever got close.

Every Thursday evening, Jimmy and a group of his closest friends got together at a different restaurant and talked about anything that took their fancy. Some of them were regulars—like Jimmy himself, Pat O'Brien, Ralph Bellamy, Lynne Overman, and Frank McHugh. Occasionally, they were joined by Eddie Foy, Jr., Frank Morgan, and George Murphy. They would vary their eating spots, partly because they liked the change and partly because they didn't want crowds around them. But whether it was Chasen's, the Brown Derby, Romanoff's, or a currently famous restaurant called Lucy's, the word would usually get out.

On one occasion, a senator came up to the stars' table and asked solemnly: "What do you fellows talk about when you meet every week?" None of the group knew the senator personally, although they knew who he was. They gave him a polite answer and said they were merely a group of friends who enjoyed chewing the fat. The senator said he was not convinced.

"I find that very difficult to believe," he told them. "There must be a reason why the same men meet every Thursday. There must be something more to it than just mere pleasantries." The senator, despite the diners' protests, went away scratching his head and muttering about there being "more to it." Wagging his finger in an almost Cagneylike pose he said: "I still find what you say hard to believe and I am going to make it my business to find out."

Despite the senator's threat the dinners went on, with week after week a different member of what Bellamy now likes to call the Boys' Club paying the check. For some time, the club had the more ominous title of the Irish Mafia—even though Bellamy's origins were English and French; Frank Morgan was by origin German (his name was really Wapperman); and Lynne Overman was Scandinavian.

Most of the group varied their menu week by week. Lynne Overman was the exception; he always demanded a hefty portion of Lyonnaise potatoes. When Overman died—the first of the Boys' Club to go—the other members met as usual the following Thursday. Pat O'Brien ordered Lyonnaise potatoes, and when they were brought he offered them around. No one wanted any. Pat was almost speechless. "What's the matter?" he asked. "You don't love Lynne? You don't want his potatoes?" The only one to speak up was Frank McHugh: "Sure I love him—but I don't want to join him."

For Jimmy, the evening out with the club was one of the few he ever spent away from home and away from Bill. She was once asked whether she enjoyed the fine life she was now able to afford. "Yes," she said. "It's swell. But Jimmy and I would be happy anywhere—sharing things."

Most important to her way of seeing things was that the System should not be allowed to change their lives. "My way is to treat Jimmy as if he were a businessman," she said. "Wave him off to the office in the morning and kiss him when he comes home." And what about the beautiful women he met daily on the set? "They're like secretaries. Just part of the job."

And she saw her job as principally to keep Jimmy happy at home and entertain his friends, who were usually her friends, too.

When Bill was hostess to Jimmy's friends at the Cagney home, the most important part of the evening would undoubtedly be her serving of the specialty of the house—Iowa stew. In fact, the culinary arts seemed to take on a particular importance when this group entertained each other. Ralph Bellamy would usually go into the kitchen himself to concoct his own favorite brand of chili, and Jimmy would use the stove, too. But neither Pat O'Brien nor Spencer Tracy usually stepped into the kitchen to do more than smell what their friends had cooked for them.

Jimmy loved his home. He loved, too, the opportunities to take Bill out into the country, where the air was unpolluted by movie-colony politics and he could avoid the public. He would have been the first to appreciate the important place his fans held in his career, and he knew that without them there would have been no money to put into the bank. But he would not pretend to like being chased by the autograph hunters. And now in the mid-1930's, he was being followed by people seeking his signature as much as that of any other superstar. On one occasion in New York, an autograph hunter chained his book to his wrist, so that it wouldn't be snatched away by anyone else in the crush.

In Jimmy's new picture, Pat O'Brien played Jimmy's brother Pat and Frank McHugh his brother Mike. Jimmy complicated matters by being called Danny, and the film called *The Irish in US*.

With Jimmy wearing a pair of boxing gloves much of the time and Mary Gordon playing the mother who could easily have doubled for his own mother, Carrie, it had just the germ of autobiography about it. Still, it came off as a disaster. Before long it grew as stale as the brogue used by Mary Gordon—which *Time* magazine said was so strong that "to the possible improvement of the picture, half her lines are virtually unintelligible."

The director, Lloyd Bacon, was probably not unaware of Cagney's reservations about the picture. Every day he would call out to Jimmy and Pat O'Brien: "Boys, the rushes are great." He did it so often that an exasperated Cagney finally rounded on Bacon: "Listen, Lloyd. If the rushes are so great why don't we forget the picture and release the rushes?" Indeed, it might not have been a bad idea.

Jimmy was still, in his way, fighting the System—winning some of the time, losing at others. He successfully protested when one script called for him to have his hands bandaged throughout the picture—supposedly because he had been doing so much fighting—and butt his opponents with his head, instead. In another picture, he refused to just go and strike a policeman without having any valid reason for doing so.

Then in 1935, an offer was made that he had no reason to want to refuse. It came from Max Reinhardt, one of the most respected names in international cinema and one of the directors who had given the German film industry its place in the world scene. When Hitler came to power, Reinhardt fled to Hollywood, and now he was offering Cagney a role that was as different from anything he had done before as Jimmy could have wished. It required him to wear, in turn, a Roman toga, a Robin Hood–style cap, and an ass's head.

Reinhardt's film was a new interpretation of *A Midsummer Night's Dream*. It turned out to be more like a midsummer nightmare with many of the pure Shakespearean lines broken up to fit the German director's idea of English poetry. The miscasting of Cagney as Bottom was matched by Mickey Rooney playing Puck, Dick Powell as Lysander, and Joe E.

Brown as Flute. Olivia de Havilland was the least disastrous in the role of Hermia. It all turned out to be a Hollywood caricature and not the artistic challenge Warner Bros. had been boasting.

But Jimmy was as enthusiastic as anyone else when the production was first mooted. Now, he thought, he would really be able to escape from all that typecasting. He was also flattered because Reinhardt thought he was knowledgeable enough to offer useful advice on various problems that cropped up during filming. But he also knew what the director meant when, after a scene, he would look in his direction and say rather scathingly: "Thank you, Mr. Cagney...." Jimmy knew what was coming next—and did the scene again.

Reinhardt was undoubtedly the most exacting director Cagney had yet worked with. But he knew when his cast needed a break. More than once he stopped shooting altogether and called out to one of his actors: "You look fatigued." At that point, someone on the set would crack a joke and Reinhardt would be the first to respond. "Good," he'd say then. "You look relaxed. You forget what you think are the gravity and restrictions of a Shakespearean role and you are yourself." Unfortunately for that picture, no one really did escape those restrictions. But Jimmy was able to appreciate that perhaps Shakespeare did have something on the Hollywood of 1935. "I am reasonably certain if the dramatist were alive today," he said, "movie producers would have asked Mr. Shakespeare to write in a scene in which I did physical violence to someone, for producers seem convinced that the public does not care for me if I don't deliver at least one punch per picture."

Jimmy delivered no punches, either on screen or to his audiences. But Shakespeare's story was the principal sufferer. Everything about the production had about it the stamp of Hollywood. The biggest sound stages in the town were used for the film—all 66,000 square feet of them. Costume designers had a field day. Not only did they have to construct a swiveling ass's head for Cagney but there had to be rubber suits for the batmen, cellophane wings for the child fairies, and frogmen's suits for the frogmen. Also, huge leaves had to be quickly converted into violins, jeweled cobwebs and moonbeams had to be able to take the patter of 108 dancing girls' feet.

When everything was seemingly right, Reinhardt thought of ways of doing much of it again. Mickey Rooney broke a leg tobogganing; a trained black bear that had to be used in several of the scenes suddenly died. Then, to complicate matters still further, two of the sets were destroyed by fire.

When it was all over, Reinhardt said he was satisfied with his results and Cagney was the "greatest of the talkie stars." He went on: "His acting gives a mysterious, dangerous and terrifying uncertainty that never allows the tenseness of an audience to relax. His reactions were unexpected, fresh, and never conventional. The part of Bottom has never been played with such uncanny artistry. The range of his genius is limitless." He was saying what critics had been saying now for years, but with Reinhardt's reputation as an "art" director the praise took on a new meaning. He said he was convinced Jimmy was "the best actor in Hollywood. Few artists have ever had his interests, his dramatic drive. Every movement of his body and his incredible hands contribute to the story he is trying to tell."

Cagney said Reinhardt made him enjoy the experience of making *A Midsummer Night's Dream* and, as a result, he was now forming a Max Reinhardt Alumni Association that would give annual charity performances of the film. Nothing more was heard of the association and there were no annual performances, much to nobody's great displeasure. Perhaps the New York *Herald Tribune* summed it up best: "Mr. Cagney is effective throughout the role because he really is a first-rate actor. At the same time, he did disappoint me slightly. I thought he would be something more than just effective." The reason is not all that difficult to perceive—for almost the first time, Jimmy had no means of bringing his Yorkville past into a picture.

Frisco Kid was much more the old Cagney. The previously faithful followers who admitted they had stayed away in droves from *A Midsummer Night's Dream* returned for *Kid*. They were glad to see him punching his way through the film in his best form, and dressed to kill after striking it rich in the California gold rush. He starts off in the picture as a penniless sailor being shanghaied in San Francisco Bay. Director Lloyd Bacon stood waist-deep in the Warner Bros. "lake" giving instructions to his assistant on just where he wanted Jimmy dropped down a staircase.

"Maybe I could take a swim first?" Jimmy asked, trying to appear unconcerned at the sort of drop usually reserved for stuntmen. "Maybe you couldn't," replied Bacon crisply. "You go around the back and climb up to the top of the stairs like a good boy—so that we can drop you through the trap door."

"You show me how," said Cagney. "You pretend you are me and I'll drop *you* down the stairs."

Bacon said he was content to wait for Jimmy's own individual interpretation of that scene.

"Action," called the director. The fog machine started and Jimmy dropped through the trap door into the water.

"How was it?" called Cagney.

"Consider yourself shanghaied," replied the director.

That was exactly how Jimmy had been feeling since he had signed his last Warner contract. He was already beginning to search for ways of once more getting out. But for the moment he had another picture to make, *Ceiling Zero*. Once again, Pat

O'Brien was his flying colleague and once again the picture showed the fine rapport that existed between them. The story line was conventional enough—about a civil aviation pilot constantly in trouble for falling down on the job, only to be recognized as a hero when he crashes testing a top-secret device. Cagney's assaults on women in the film were mostly verbal: "Yeh, married five years. Wanna see the scars?"

In London, the *Daily Mail* said: "This is undoubtedly one of the finest films ever to come out of Hollywood." The New York *Evening Post*'s Thornton Delehanty said Cagney's portrait of the pilot was "remarkably accurate." That could also have been a reasonable interpretation of the way he judged the current situation in Hollywood. He had now made up his mind once again to formalize his state of war with Warner Bros.

11 CITY FOR CONQUEST

It was a matter of opinion as to who had the more right on their side, James Cagney or Warner Bros. The situation embodied the law of physics that was later to become a popular song—the irresistible force meeting the immovable object. One of them had to give, but no one knew which it would be.

Cagney still felt he was being exploited. Warner Bros.—mainly in the form of Jack L.—still pointed to its contract with the star. According to their lawyers, it left no doubt that they were in a position to demand more work without paying the actor an additional cent. After all, they were paying him over $3000 a week now that the extras in the contract were beginning to come into force. The studio felt they were entitled to a stand. Cagney, on the other hand, pointed out that his pictures were making something like $1,500,000 each and he was being asked to make no more than four films a year; the studio was asking him to make five.

Ten years later, wags were to dub the Warner studio of the 1930's the "Buchenwald of Burbank." In 1935, however, Jack

Warner and his colleagues were looking very self-righteous. Their big mistake was to ask James Cagney to play a professional baseball player in their film *Over the Wall*. Jimmy said that if he made that film he would never again be able to turn down a project he didn't like, and before long the public would show its own displeasure. "It doesn't make any difference how competent an actor you may be," he said. "If the public doesn't want to see you any more, you're all washed up."

His mind made up, he declared he was not going to make *Over the Wall* under any circumstances. Neither was he going to make any other Warner Bros. pictures until they agreed to pay him $4500 a week. It was not that he needed the extra money; he just wanted Jack Warner to know he couldn't be exploited. Thanks to Warner Bros., Cagney had, indeed, made enough to finally achieve the ambition born in him when he had visited his great-aunt in Brooklyn at age five. He bought a farm.

It was at Martha's Vineyard, an island off the Cape Cod coastline in Massachusetts, and Jimmy saw it mainly as a place that was far from the pressures of Burbank and one that only a few people had heard of. He and Bill had made the discovery only after an extensive search of other properties in the state as well as in Maine, Vermont, and Pennsylvania. When he saw the Martha's Vineyard farm and the two-hundred-year-old house that went with it, he realized he had found what he had been looking for. Years later, he was to explain: "I stood there and thought: 'Here it is. Here it is. To live on a farm, surrounded by salt water—that's the top. The best there is.' "

They moved into the house even before the extensive reconstruction work that was necessary had begun. There they were able to forget the studio, listen to the birds, and smell the soil that was so different from anything near a sound stage. If there were going to be any frustrations about being so far away from where things were happening, he could give vent to them all on a new tractor. He and Bill also had a yacht. As a mark of affection for the Vineyard, Jimmy called the boat the *Martha.*

When Warner Bros. finally decided to issue a statement about their latest fracas with Cagney, they had to reveal that they could not reach their renegade star. He was sailing on the ocean. The studio was left with practically nothing to say except that Jimmy was "temporarily off the payroll."

To help Jimmy with his fight, there was the now ever-present figure of his youngest brother Bill, his business manager. William Cagney was heavier than his brother and the almost angelic expression he constantly wore gave a false impression that he was easy to walk over. Thinking that was the biggest mistake Warner Bros. made in its fight with his brother. Bill was prepared to hold out where Jimmy would have caved in. The younger Cagney was every bit as tough in the executive offices as the older one was on the screen.

With Bill's blessing, Jimmy's lawyers now filed suit to cancel the contract with the studio. Asked why, Jimmy put it bluntly: "I've been overworked. I've made ten pictures in the years 1934–35." He had an additional problem: the other Hollywood studios were blacklisting him. It was not so much that the System was uniting against him as a threat of Warner's slapping lawsuits on anyone giving Cagney work.

The Superior Court ruled that Warner Bros. had now to "show cause why they should not be restrained from interfering with [Cagney's] efforts to obtain other employment." The legal battle was on, with the studio now trying to find a "cause" that would be acceptable.

Jimmy, meanwhile, revealed that he had been having talks with Sir Michael Balcon, head of the large London studio Gaumont British. He did not know what part Balcon had in mind for him, he said, but it wouldn't be a gangster role.

"Tough-guy roles are unpopular in Britain, I know they alienate British audiences, and I definitely will not continue to play them." He could possibly have had in mind a recent poll conducted by the British cinema owner Sidney Bernstein, whose 124,837 patrons had been asked to state their most popular and most disliked stars. The most liked was George Arliss. The least popular were Mae West and James Cagney. The outcome of that poll probably had more to do with Mr. Bernstein's failure to get any Cagney films to show—they went to the bigger circuits—than the tastes of audiences for gangster films.

William Cagney was also coming up with ideas for Jimmy to consider. One of them was the result of a conversation with Darryl Zanuck, who had now left Warner Bros. to head the newly amalgamated Twentieth Century-Fox. "There's a possibility of a contract with Zanuck if Warner Bros. releases him," said Bill. When Warner's heard that they decided that the supreme test had now come. If they allowed Cagney to make films for anyone else, even by officially "lending" him, it would really be the end of the System. They decided to keep fighting in the courts and try to prove that their contract with Cagney was all the "cause" they needed to show.

While he waited for the court's decision, Jimmy decided to rush into nothing new. Instead, he continued to learn how to use a plow, went sailing, and thought once more about the good things in life that he could do if he were not a film star. He didn't talk any more about being a doctor, but he could think about working on the stage and pursuing an acting career far removed from the pressures of Hollywood.

Soon he announced he was going to join the world-famous Abbey Players in Dublin. No one really knew whether he was serious or not. The Abbey was pleased to hear it had been considered, but a newsman's inquiry was the first it knew of the idea. "Until our attention was drawn to this by an American paper," said a spokesman for the company, "we had not the remotest notion of his reported desire to join us. It is possible, I suppose, that he may communicate with us." He didn't. For a time he contented himself with saying for quotation that he considered the Abbey Players to be "the greatest actors in the world."

He said nothing more about going to Dublin, but his next idea was not far removed from that thought: he was going to form a repertory company of Irish actors, possibly putting the other members of the Boys' Club to work. Cagney himself, Frank McHugh, and Pat O'Brien were going to be among a company he was forming to tour towns that had populations of 100,000 or less. The first likely title would be *Playboy of the Western World* by J. M. Synge. For the moment, Pat O'Brien said he had heard no more about this idea than the Abbey had heard of the earlier suggestion, but, like them, thought it was a very good one.

Jimmy was trying to give the impression that he had everything organized. "I have a cast fairly well lined up in my mind," he said. "The next thing is to see if we can arrange it. I'd like to tour this country, then take the play to Ireland and England. We might even make a film of it later, either abroad or here."

For the moment, he was determined he wouldn't make a film for Warner Bros. He said he had good reason to take the stand: William Cagney had found a suburban cinema advertising *Ceiling Zero* with Pat O'Brien's name billed over Jimmy's. That was, he asserted, entirely against the terms of the contract. Pat and Jimmy were the closest of friends, and normally he wouldn't dream of making an issue over the question of a division of billing between them, but he did need excuses. It now seemed that he had one that was heaven-sent, and Pat realized it. There was still no doubt that had Pat been in any kind of trouble, Jimmy would have been the first to offer a hand.

The Superior Court judge said he had only one point he considered worth investigating: Was Cagney being asked to make too many films in too short a time? He deliberated and then came to a conclusion: Yes, he was. Ten films, the judge decided, was one too many in the years 1934–35.

When Jimmy heard the news he was perhaps a little surprised. "Gosh," he said when the judgment eventually reached Martha's Vineyard. "That ends a long headache for me." As for the future, perhaps he would think over Sir Michael Balcon's offer in London. He would be going there on vacation and perhaps it would all be settled then.

That would not, however, be the end of the dispute. Jack Warner said he was not going to allow the Professional Againster to win, and he was going to fight as strongly as he possibly could. Still, Cagney was undoubtedly Warner Bros.' most valuable asset, and when a bunch of studio executives met each year to plan their advertising budget for the following twelve months, his films always got the biggest slice. In 1937, when the last Cagney films made before the row were being shown, half of Warner's $5 million recorded net profit had come from Jimmy's movies. The fact that he still didn't think he was getting enough of that money for himself was, they decided, beside the point.

The studio announced it was going to appeal—and until the appeal was heard, Jimmy would not be allowed to work for any other Hollywood studio, or indeed for anyone else. But a feeler was put out to him. How much might he consider to come back amicably? He said that an extra $100,000 a year would be near the mark.

The Warner-Cagney dispute had split Hollywood more than any other single issue in the history of the film business.

Warner Bros. let no one forget that it was defending the System. "If it's us today, it could be you tomorrow," said Jack Warner, and everyone producing films knew what he meant. On the other side of the fight were the Hollywood actors, who nearly all regarded James Cagney as their standard bearer.

In London, the issue was of more academic interest. There, Sir Michael Balcon clarified the offer he had previously made to Jimmy: he wanted him to play an American serving in the British Army. Critic Campbell Dixon wrote in the London *Daily Telegraph* that he considered Cagney to be "among the great performers of the world."

For the moment, Jimmy decided to spend some time on the farm. "You know, it really is an art to do nothing," he joked. He tried it and then decided he would probably prefer to learn to ride. He said he was looking for a "nice quiet stallion" and then he would search for a couple more tractors, too. He also had to sort out the plumbing problems in the old farmhouse, but if he worried about them, he never showed it. There was also the comforting thought that the local taxes amounted to no more than $36 a year.

The Cagneys also made themselves known to the other residents of the Vineyard, mostly to assure them that they had nothing to worry about. Jimmy did his best to explain he was neither a conventional film star nor a gangster. He and Bill went sailing and sat around the house listening to the radio—"sometimes as late as eleven o'clock," as they joked. But the gangster image was hard to live down. Bill constantly found herself explaining to neighbors that her husband was "a real softie." She was doubly glad when an old friend came to visit and talked about his pal, "Soft-hearted Sam."

It seemed that Jimmy was really living the quiet country existence and liking it so much that he didn't care whether he ever made another film. Then suddenly, he was spotted leaving a train in New York and taking a taxi to the Barbizon Plaza Hotel. He was later noticed rushing into the hotel's reception area with his hat pulled down sharply over one eye.

The hotel was playing it cool over the arrival of its celebrated guest. "I can't put you through to Mr. Cagney," the manager told callers. Then he added: "Mr. Cagney isn't registered here and those are his orders to the whole world. He said he wouldn't stay here if people could get him to the telephone."

In Hollywood, however, the mystery was beginning to lift. Correspondents there were told that a new film company had been set up, the Grand National Pictures Corporation. Their president was the hitherto unknown Edward Alperson, and he was pleased to announce that his first major star had just signed a contract in New York. "Yes," said Mr. Alperson, "he *is* James Cagney."

Jack Warner felt he had been made to look a fool. As for Alperson, he was quite delighted to have beaten a previously hallowed Hollywood tradition by taking on a major studio and winning. Warner Bros. said they still considered Cagney to be their star, but Alperson said he had a contract and was going to pay Jimmy $120,000 for every film he made for Grand National. Cagney had agreed to make two films for a start and there was an understanding that there would be more. In December 1936, Alperson revealed the title of the first Cagney picture: *Great Guy*. It would also be the first film made by Grand National.

Alperson introduced his most valuable asset at a party at the New York Athletic Club, not the kind of place Jimmy would have visited when he lived in the city, and he hardly felt at home now. He found himself a chair in a corner and hoped he could sit there, without anyone's taking too much notice. A bevy of women reporters, however, gathered around him—

looking, said one onlooker, as though they all wanted to have grapefruit pushed into their pretty faces. But if Cagney did not like press receptions, he did approve of one particular aspect of his agreement with Alperson: he was being given full approval of all scripts.

While talks between Cagney and Alperson proceeded in a pleasant enough atmosphere, Warner Bros. took their case to the Appeals Court. They held that their own contract with the star was still valid and hoped the previous judgment of the Superior Court could be overturned. It was, as writer Max Breen put it at the time, "a kind of cinematic musical chairs with the films as the chairs and the Appeals Court as the man at the piano." Just in case "the man at the piano" struck an off-key note, Jimmy signed a contract for a radio series—publicizing toilet soap for $3000 an hour.

Meanwhile, magazines were running stories headed "Cagney's Back." He was not, however, back in form. If Jimmy had approved *Great Guy* as his first vehicle, he undoubtedly was mostly concerned with the opportunity it gave him to attack Warner Bros. The story, about a retired boxer who becomes a weights-and-measures inspector to trap the swindlers in New York big business, was among the weakest in his career. He certainly did not like the film's title. "People might think it is an estimate of myself," he told Alperson. "In too many films I've been made to look a bumptious braggart. I'm not that way at all. I believe audiences have confused my real character with the parts I've played."

Grand National refused to change the title. They said it represented their assessment of both James Cagney in real life and the character he played in the film. They were prepared to compromise, however; when the movie was shown in England, they called it *The Pluck of the Irish*.

Making the film was to prove easier than showing it. Grand

National may have thought Jack Warner's nose had been rubbed in the dirt when it signed up James Cagney—but it did not take into account the power he held over the exhibitors. Warner Bros. controlled about 900 important theaters in the United States and could influence the owners of a good many more. For months, the film could not get on the road at all; when it finally was shown, the number of cinemas playing *Great Guy* was very small indeed.

Despite this problem, Grand National proudly announced its next Cagney film. It would be a musical, and the old hoofer would be back doing what he appeared to like to do best. Unfortunately, *Something to Sing About* was anything but—and playing a bandleader going to Hollywood hardly did Cagney justice. But there were some spectacular scenes—including one where he prances down a staircase that just happens to look like a giant xylophone. He strums a guitar, jokes, and makes love to Evelyn Daw and Mona Barrie. *Variety* commented: "Cagney had brushed up on his tapping and handles himself easily and with assurance."

Certainly he was dancing better than at any other time—possibly with joy at not having Jack Warner breathing down his neck. All the time he was working on the film, there was the usual determination to regard it as the most important thing that had ever happened on a sound stage.

The moment that he stopped filming *Something to Sing About* at what had been the old Pathé studio, he was on a train back to Martha's Vineyard. Once there, he had the phonograph going and was practicing his dancing until he could almost feel the pounds falling away. Hoofing was the best way he knew of cutting down his weight.

The farm was also a good place to escape some of the pressures of Hollywood. Stories had been circulating about him having rows with his new studio. "I'm not a malcontent," he protested and he hoped his public would believe him. But the stories were not entirely about his relationship with producers. Ever since the Steffens affair, right-wing elements had been trying to keep alive the tag of "Cagney the Red." Every now and then, they would find what they took to be evidence backing their theories—and the shouting could be heard loudest of all when Cagney agreed to head a $300,000 fund to help the Spanish Republican Government in the Civil War, which was now being lost to General Franco's rebels. Jimmy insisted the controversy did not bother him, and promptly announced that Errol Flynn had joined their number and was going out to Spain to photograph the fighting. When he returned, Flynn would be in a position to advise on the best use to which the money collected by the film colony could be put.

The row over the fund was followed by an announcement by the ultraright-wing Knights of Columbus that they were about to "investigate" James Cagney and Fredric March, who had also backed the appeal.

There were still people, however, who were not afraid of talking about "my friend James Cagney." When Jimmy went on a tour of Washington, he was treated with something of the pomp usually reserved for a head of state. No one was prouder showing him around the federal buildings than his own congressman, Representative John M. Costello of Hollywood. Before Jimmy went on his tour, the congressman got him to sit down and write autographs on the pages of a pad—which he then tore out and handed to all who wanted them. Most of those in the crowd did.

No one would have been happier than Grand National Pictures to have James Cagney's autograph—on a new contract. But in January 1938, they were forced to announce that their star was leaving them. The agreement with Cagney was being terminated "by mutual consent"—and as far as they knew, he was going back to Warner Bros.

The game of musical chairs was over. The California Appeals Court finally considered Warner Bros.' request to set aside the earlier judgment and came out solidly in favor of the studio—and the System. Cagney's contract with Warner Bros. had been "good," the court decided, and the studio had every right to expect its former number one star to go back to work for it.

Jack Warner now seemed much more keen to be on good terms with the "Professional Againster" than Jimmy was to be friendly with him. Cagney probably would have been happy just to work on his farm. Warner, however, was thinking of the box office: the announcement of a new Cagney film was enough to guarantee standing-room-only business.

The two parties had to be brought together somehow, and the means of doing so turned out to be Pat O'Brien, who had never escaped the System but was still a very close fried of Jimmy's. With O'Brien acting as go-between, Cagney and Warner shook hands and made up. Warner promised a new contract that would guarantee a better deal with every picture —and as a consequence a new look to his career. James Cagney was once more a Warner Bros. star—and this time he was going to be treated like one.

12 SMART MONEY

JAMES CAGNEY always knew how much he was worth. When he agreed to do his first Warner Bros. film in two years for $150,000, he did not think how lucky he was. The way he saw it, he was giving Jack Warner and his brother Harry full value for their money. At the same time, Jimmy made no attempt to squeeze anything more from the studio. His view of his own status was no more inflated now than it had ever been; he never displayed any prima donna antics. His wife was still "his girl Bill," and he had no desire to take up with hopeful starlets.

His idea of bliss was getting up before six and driving his tractor on the farm. Luxury was standing at the helm of his boat, the *Martha*. Even so, he didn't always manage to forsake the life of a film actor. Once, when he thought he had sailed far away from civilization, he came across a film crew and offered them any expertise they thought he might have. The filmmakers decided they did have use for him—as an extra. A very careful look at the Charles Laughton-Clark Gable version of *Mutiny on the Bounty* might reveal James Cagney running along the deck of Captain Bligh's ship. Even with his own supercharged powers of observation, Jimmy has never been able to spot himself in it.

At the back of Jimmy's mind was always the feeling that whatever success he had achieved he owed to his audience. It was for their sake that he would never think of coasting along with a part. His work always had to be the best because, if it were not, perhaps even Warner Bros. would not want him any more. He was still only thirty-eight, but he was never certain what the following day would bring.

He never ceased to wonder at the power and money he had. In 1938, he was more aware than ever of the changes brought by time. He went back to Yorkville, and found it very different from the Yorkville he had known. New apartment houses had gone up where the tenements and near-slums had been. It was in one of these luxury buildings on East Eighty-sixth Street that he and Bill visited Dorothy Parker. The humorist thought he would be intrigued by the changes in the district. When they surveyed the scene from her penthouse window, Jimmy confessed he was speechless. "I don't know anything that has stirred me as deeply as that," he said afterward. "This is a great city." In later years, he was to change that view of New York quite considerably. But in 1938, East Eighty-sixth Street was a very much smarter place to be than he had once thought possible, and mugging was neither a word nor an experience most people knew.

He made frequent visits to his old home town, and on each trip felt more proud of "this great city." His mother, sister, and brothers had long since left their old home, but he still felt part of the "Cagney Clan." He was never more proud than on the day in May 1938 when Jeanne Cagney, holder of a Phi Beta Kappa key, was graduated from Hunter College—the very same Hunter College that had once called on his help with its drama productions. Sitting in the audience, he was treated in true celebrity style.

When he arrived back in Hollywood to begin his first film covered by the new contract, the welcome was even more generous. The only people in Los Angeles who seemed less than happy at his return were Grand National. Without their big star they would soon go out of business, and they already knew it.

Before they announced the name of Jimmy's new film, Warner Bros. decided to take him on a nationwide publicity tour—just in case, they thought, anyone had forgotten who he was. Cagney did not take to that idea any more happily than he would have at any other time in his career, but he recognized it as part of the penance of being a professional.

The movie was to be *Boy Meets Girl,* which had been a very successful Broadway comedy about life in Hollywood. The studio promised Jimmy a 10 per cent commission on takings on top of his agreed fee, as a gesture of the esteem in which they held him. In the movie, Cagney and Pat O'Brien play two script writers fighting the ego of a big star. They play practical jokes on the actor—and, dressed in unbelievably long overcoats and berets, look rather like a couple of practical jokes themselves. Ronald Reagan has a brief role in the movie, playing an announcer at a major studio premiere, and the romantic interest comes in the form of a slight blonde called Marie Wilson. The Warner Bros. publicity department notified the public that Miss Wilson had once written James Cagney a fan letter, and still slept with the reply under her pillow.

The film was a nice fluffy piece of nonsense of which Howard Barnes wrote in the New York *Herald Tribune:* "It is the performing rather than the adaptation or the direction which has succeeded in changing a popular stage farce into an extremely amusing screen comedy."

Cagney was pleased. He had scored as a comedian without having to either give a message or deliver a punch. Writing in *Stars and Films* in 1938, Foster Clark—he headed his article "A Highbrow Looks at Cagney"—said: "The fiery, brilliant redhead appeals to people other than those who just like to see a tough guy in action. His body is a transparent instrument for the demonstration of every facet of the lives of millions of men into whose class he was born. He is not only a roughneck from a downtown filling station nor a worn-out racing driver, nor a cocky truckman nor a damn good prize fighter, nor a petty gangster, nor a traveling salesman, nor a picture-snatcher, but all of these varied characters, each perfectly realized in itself with inimitable addition of his own brand (since he was born with it) of recklessness, bitterness, anguished comedy and sober, hysterical gaiety."

More importantly, he went on: "Cagney is the perfect portrait of the American urban man and boy whose life is so insecure and dangerous that the only buckler they can forge for themselves up to the present has been in the anarchic, ruthless, funny and tender violence which is apparent (as their reflection) in his every gesture. His walk, his nervous fists, his abrupt silences and his steady mounting rage."

People from all kinds of backgrounds were sharing those sentiments, even if they did not choose to use that sort of language. But in September 1938, public concern focused on a different sentiment. They thought Jimmy was dead.

A massive hurricane had hit the Cape Cod area, and by all accounts Martha's Vineyard was hit hardest of all. It was feared that 60,000 people in the area were homeless, and at least 600 were known to be dead. Early reports listed Jimmy and Bill and their neighbor Walter Huston as being among the dead. Eyewitnesses said they could not possibly have survived the carnage. The damage to property was said to have reached millions of dollars. Jimmy and Bill were known to have been at the farm when the hurricane struck and it seemed unlikely they could have survived. Warner Bros. sadly admitted they had been unable to contact them.

For days, there was no news. Finally, a fisherman managed to sail from Cape Cod and get a message to a grocery delivery boy. The boy passed it to a man in Boston and the man, one of Jimmy's friends, phoned Burbank. The Cagneys were safe and well, he said, and their home had been only slightly damaged. Jimmy later revealed that he had used the time that he was marooned to practice his riding. There was talk of his making a Western, and he thought there was no better way of learning how to ride for a film than doing it in the worst possible conditions.

First, however, there was a more urgent movie commitment. It was to be *Angels with Dirty Faces,* a film from which both Warner Bros. and James Cagney would emerge with very much enhanced international reputations. If Jimmy had put chunks of his own life into movies before, now he was laying out his soul for public inspection, too. The "angels" were just the type with whom he used to chat and fight in Yorkville. Any one of the "dirty faces" could have been his own. He was telling a story he knew better than anyone else in Hollywood. As he explained, "If you've never been poor, you've cut yourself off from half of humanity."

The movie was the story of two tough East Side youths who get up to the sort of tricks which that environment seemed to breed. One of them, played by Pat O'Brien, escapes and becomes a priest. The other, played by Cagney, is caught, is infected with the poison of gangs and prison cells, and turns into a criminal. The criminal retains his friendship for the priest and his love for the girl next door (played by a delicious Ann Sheridan). He is also a hero for the Dead End Kids, the gang led by Leo Gorcey, who would eventually call themselves the Bowery Boys.

Cagney is a braggart, and the boys, who would spend all their time in the gutter were it not for Father O'Brien and his basketball court, regard everything he says as undiluted wisdom. Cagney the gangster is as true to their way of life as the trash cans in the street. Any other actor would merely have accepted the script writer's "Hi, there" greeting to the boys. Instead, Jimmy said: "What da ya hear? What da ya say?" He had been saving that for the right occasion, and now that occasion had arrived.

The tough kid with the unique form of speech was not the only Yorkville character brought to new life in the film. In *Angels with Dirty Faces,* for the first and only time in his career, Jimmy hitched his trousers and nervously twitched his head and shoulders. That, too, he had been saving for just the right moment—and because he felt the moment had come, an episode was added to the history of the film. Ever since *Angels with Dirty Faces,* hundreds of impersonators have been copying the man Cagney insists was really a pimp in an electric-blue suit standing on a street corner in Yorkville.

His experience showed itself not just on the screen, but on the set before the cameras started turning. Jimmy was having a run-through on the basketball court with the Dead End Kids. One of the boys was constantly trying to hit Pat O'Brien with a ball when he was not looking. "If he tries that again, Paddy," said Cagney, "just watch. . . ." It did happen again, and Jimmy hit the boy under the chin. "Remember that," he told the shocked kid. "The next time, I'll deck you."

The real impact of *Angels with Dirty Faces* comes at the end, when Cagney is condemned to the electric chair for murder. His priest friend begs him for one last request—to go to his death screaming for mercy. If the papers could report that the big tough guy died a coward, he argues, the dirty-faced angels might be disillusioned about the life of crime.

Cagney protests, but does meet his friend's request. He had to be dragged to the chair, shouting and screaming as he had never been seen to do before. It was a magnificent performance, but as soon as the take was over, the hysterical Cagney wiped the sweat off his brow and went to chat with a bunch of friends waiting behind the camera.

"How you do eet, Jeemy, I do not onnerstand," said the Hungarian-born director, Michael Curtiz. "Crying one moment, laughing the next."

"Easy, Mike," explained Cagney. "You're an amateur actor. I'm a professional."

It was a title most critics were happy to bestow. Rose Pelswick wrote in the New York *Journal American* that Jimmy had been given "a role tailored to his measure and [he] checks in a performance that's swift and sure and electrical." Pat O'Brien was playing his best role to date and giving a performance to justify it. Humphrey Bogart (who was older than Jimmy, but whose career took a lot longer to get off the ground) showed promise in the role of a shyster lawyer.

The London *Sunday Express* said of *Angels:* "James Cagney takes the picture into his two small but active fists and crashes its melodrama home with all the force of a punching on the backswing." And another British critic, Seton Margrave, said in the *Daily Mail:* "James Cagney is back in one of the best performances of his film life. Once again, he is acting like a human dynamo. I like his direct, vigorous style of acting. It is uncompromising, stimulating like a March wind, and I cannot see him too often."

As if to consummate the praise being heaped upon him for what was undoubtedly the finest Cagney film to date, the New York Film Critics gave him their annual Critics Award. He was voted "the actor of the year who gave the finest performance of the year." But the award was confirmed only on the ninth ballot, and he had to share the honors with Margaret Sullavan for her part in *Three Comrades.*

While everyone else was cheering another Cagney triumph, Jimmy was once more giving vent to all his old doubts. "The public will grow sick of that man I play on the screen if they see me year after year characterizing him again and again," he said. And then he added a touch of the old vitriol: "The studio will have made a great deal of money out of me but when I'm through, I won't be worth a nickel to myself."

Now he was thinking not so much about putting groceries on the table as being able to live with himself. And he still resented the fact that "the good-looking guys" were earning more than the $150,000 a picture—plus 10 per cent—that the studio was paying him. "They have audience appeal and sympathy the moment they appear on the screen; I, on the other hand, have to use every scrap of acting in me to put across even the simplest scene. My stories have to be strong and I feel there aren't enough strong pictures about." When he was asked what sort of movie he really fancied for himself, he replied: "I just want to wear a uniform."

Instead, Warner Bros. decided it was time for that cowboy suit. The film would be *The Oklahoma Kid,* but although he wore a Stetson and cowboy boots, it was much like any other Cagney film. He didn't really have the right Western accent, and he shot his guns as though he were worried about a ricochet from a skyscraper. He punched in the Wild West in the same way he did on the East Side, with his face screwed into the same kind of grimace.

But his practice, riding the horses at Martha's Vineyard, showed. In the studio, he learned how to sit on the Western saddle and how to mount it—by clutching the saddle horn with both hands and then lifting himself. Over the fields, he had practiced a "flying mount" while the horse was in motion. In the studio a former cavalryman, who had served under General Pershing in the Mexican Wars, taught him how to shoot from a moving horse. A real cowboy demonstrated how to "flip a leg" over a horse without hurting either himself or the animal with his spurs—and how in one movement to take off his ten-gallon hat to a lady and put it on again. In early 1939, when the film was made, it was still important to know how to take off your hat to a lady. Humphrey Bogart was again Cagney's principal supporting player—this time, his rival in love.

Jimmy had no pretensions about *The Oklahoma Kid,* but he thought it was a vital ingredient in his career. "Any American actor," he said at the time, "should be ready to tote a gun and ride a horse. Westerns are basically an important aspect of American history." Years later, however, he recognized the film had been "something of a fiasco. Bogart and me on what you might call new territory, stalking around the set like a couple of city slickers dolled up in Western rigout."

The man who had done so much for grapefruit a few years before now used tomato ketchup in much the same way—hurling it at anyone who looked as if he might want a fight. Audiences seemed to like it more than the critics. Twelve years later in *Sight and Sound* an anonymous editorial writer explained Cagney's appeal in *The Oklahoma Kid:* "It is safe to say that if Cagney had been four inches taller, his popularity would be fathoms less than it is. Villains before him tended to be huge. They loomed and slobbered. You could see them coming. Cagney was and is spruce, dapper and grinning. When he hits a friend over the ear with a revolver butt, he does it as casually as he will presently press the elevator button."

In the London *Daily Express,* Paul Holt said the film was "phony" but then added: "I love phony films." The censors did not, however. The Ohio censorship board sent a young lady to meet Jimmy. "Why do you make your characters so attractive?" this "gal," as Cagney described her, asked. Jimmy replied by quoting his old idol, Lowell Sherman: "You've got to sprinkle the goodies along the way. Anything people laugh at, they can't hate," he told her.

In 1938 Cagney was the highest-paid star in the movie industry. The $234,000 he had earned was $9000 more than Kay Francis had been paid, and it was the first time Jimmy had figured anywhere in the charts. Since Hollywood was paying more than any other industry, Jimmy was also America's biggest salary earner that year. The highest figure outside of the film business was the $200,000 earned by Richard R. Dupree, president of Procter & Gamble, the soap empire.

Who earned the most money was easily worked out, because all the studios filed their figures for public inspection. Who would make which film was not so easily settled. Every year, the studios issued glossy full-color brochures giving details of the films they were planning to make in the coming twelve months. But no one took them seriously. Although they showed pictures of stars about to take leading roles in exciting new movies, it was well known that most of them never would. The pictures were the figments of a publicity man's vivid imagination. But with stars on the payroll and getting vast salaries the studios had to show their stockholders that they would be making the fullest use of them.

In February 1939, Warner Bros. announced it was going to star James Cagney in the life story of John Dillinger. They were calling it *Dillinger—Outlaw,* and it would, they said, be their answer to Twentieth Century-Fox's *Jesse James.* A month later, they said that instead of Cagney, Humphrey Bogart would star in the film. Four weeks later, Warner Bros. revealed the film would be called *The Life of John Dillinger* and would have

George Raft in the starring part. Five weeks on, it again was postponed. Eventually, it reached the screen in 1945, with Lawrence Tierney in the title role.

Warner Bros. had announced that it was relieving Jimmy of the Dillinger role because, in the carefully phrased words of the publicity machine, he was being allowed to "go soft." He was needed, they said, for a new musical called *On Your Toes*. But he would not make that either. Instead, they announced that Cagney would appear in *John Paul Jones* and play the title role of the man known as the Father of the American Navy. "Picture Cagney," said a publicity handout, "as that fiery scourge of the sea, whose daring conquest led America through the stormiest naval encounters of the Revolutionary War." But audiences could do no more than picture it in their minds. *John Paul Jones* was also dropped from the shooting schedules.

While the studios were trying to work out exactly which film Jimmy would be making, newspapermen were still trying to work out why he should be working at all. "His own mother would hardly call him handsome," said the *Daily Telegraph* in London. "His face is craggy and square, his figure is stocky. His voice is crisp rather than musical. Yet how effortlessly he holds the eye and ear—even when, at one memorable occasion, he breaks into song and dance. Dump him down with his back to the camera and Hedy Lamarr playing opposite him and I wager your eyes would still be riveted on the electrical little man with red hair."

"Why?" asked the *Telegraph*. "It is easy to mumble something about personality. Personality, he certainly possesses to an extraordinary degree. But that is only half Mr. Cagney's secret. He happens also to be an actor—by any reasonable standards, one of the finest on the screen. He has a razor-edged intelligence that enables him to get under the skin of G-men and gangsters and Shakespearean clowns—a nonchalant sincerity that can be very moving and a complete mastery of the medium. As a technician, he is brilliant. Not even the late Gerald du Maurier could achieve a greater effort with a line apparently thrown away and his timing is superb.

"He delivers a line as a first-class boxer delivers a punch. We all know the amateur ominously drawing back glove and shoulder to start the punch that is meant to be annihilating —and would be if it landed from somewhere in the neighborhood of the right heel. The champion packs more wallop into a blow delivered without warning from a range of perhaps eight inches. In the idiom of the ring, he does not telegraph his punches. It is the same with Mr. Cagney. No matter how good a line, he puts it over casually and subtly without the triumphant overemphasis, the 'just-wait-till-you-hear-this-one' leer that makes so many screen dialogues sound like a vaudeville act one knows by heart."

If the sophisticated critics liked Cagney and his work, the same could not be said about a group of tradesmen in the tiny town of St. Ives in Cornwall, England. Mr. Percy Browning, a retired dairyman, Mr. R. H. Hope, a trade unionist who was now more than seventy years old, and Mr. Harry Male, the former local postmaster, were the local film licensing committee. They had been asked to give *Angels with Dirty Faces* their approval, but decided to ban it. They did not realize that at a time when the cinema was going through one of its worst slumps, publicity of their action guaranteed the film record business everywhere else it played in Britain. Just before the outbreak of the Second World War, America—and New York in particular—represented a certain kind of paradise for a lot of glamour-starved Britons. They were not the least bit bothered that its angels happened to have dirty faces.

Jimmy and Bill had bought themselves a new house in Beverly Hills. Most of their nonworking time would be spent, they had decided, in Martha's Vineyard. But the home on Coldwater Canyon—with a nice stretch of farmland nearby—was handy "for the shop." It wouldn't be easy to commute between the Warner lot at Burbank and New England—and in the winter, even a farm-loving boy like Cagney found the California weather kinder than the snows of the East. Their new home, high in the hills, would be convenient for Sunset Boulevard, and he would have no trouble getting to work on time—something he always insisted upon doing.

But building the house had its problems. Jimmy said he wanted a squat stone-and-timber home with nine-foot ceilings downstairs and those on the second floor no more than eight feet high. But the builder said it could not be done. In California, the local rule was the ceilings had to be the same height both up and downstairs—and there had to be a sloping roof. Cagney bowed to authority; the house went up as the regulations stipulated, and is still today the principal Cagney California residence—at the top of a long steep drive, with only a letterbox at the side of the road to show there is a house there at all.

Jimmy was very proud because it was the first home he had ever owned that didn't have a clothesline showing—that was hidden neatly behind the garage. The house itself was not the least pretentious, unlike most people's idea of a film star's home—and none of the tours of the stars' residences have ever been allowed to include it on their itineraries. There were just two bedrooms, a kitchen, a dining room, living room, and a library.

Bill's one peccadillo was to install a fourposter bed. Jimmy at first was not sure he liked the idea quite as much as she did; but months before they moved in, Bill even managed to persuade him to accept the ruffles she had designed for the bottom of the bed. Jimmy took it no harder than he had some of the other more serious problems of Hollywood. But he had his own ideas incorporated into the house, too. He put in a collection of pipes—even though he didn't smoke. He also had an antique cobbler's bench—and hastened to assure visitors that he didn't make shoes, either.

The new house was convenient not only for the studio; it was also handy for Balboa Island, where Jimmy now anchored the *Martha*. Almost any day, he and Bill could be seen driving off in their roadster, bound for the island.

All was not peaceful in the film town, however, and Jimmy was in the thick of things once more. Sophie Tucker, who proudly billed herself as "The Last of the Red Hot Mamas," announced she was leading the American Federation of Actors—an organization which had been expelled from the Associated Actors and Artists of America. There had been charges of mismanagement, but Sophie was determined to stay with them, despite protests from James Cagney, who thought it was unprofessional and told her so. Miss Tucker, however, said she was going to affiliate her group with the Stagehands Union, despite Jimmy's objection. "I've been up against big billing before," she declared.

As always, Jimmy was much more concerned about his own family. The happiest news he had heard in a long time was that his mother and sister were now moving to Los Angeles. They had taken an apartment in the city's business district with Ed Cagney, and Jeanne was going into films.

Jeanne Cagney was just over twenty now, and every appearance she had made on the amateur stage had shown she possessed considerable talent. She was also an expert linguist and spoke French as though she were born in France. The family seemed to think she would be a teacher, but it was a film career she said she wanted first—on the condition that Jimmy didn't help her. "My brother got to the top without any pull, and that's what I hope to do," she said. Jeanne had been spotted by a talent scout at one of her shows, and she landed a part in the film *All Women Have Secrets*. One of those secrets that she tried to keep on the set was that she had a brother called James Cagney.

Carrie was showing all the pride of an Irish mother whose son has done what he wanted to do, and done it well. But she was not sure about his image. When she started meeting people in the film world after her move to the Coast, she would always say: "I suppose you know my gangster son?" She was not entirely joking. Just before leaving New York she had read in a newspaper about James Cagney once being a real hoodlum.

"I had to read it six times," she said. "I thought maybe they had the wrong name in the magazine. Not long after, I read another story about his early life, and I almost cried. I was going to write Jimmy about it, but I thought: 'Oh, well, next month they'll have something else to say.' But they didn't. Why, even a billboard for one picture said that Jimmy was playing himself —a regular modern outlaw."

As she knew, Jimmy was really himself when he was on the farm. But the studio wouldn't let him stay there.

13 THE FIGHTING 69TH

CAGNEY was now over forty and by all accounts happier than he had been at any time in his career. He and Jack Warner were still far from good friends, but making his stand had produced the results he wanted. He did not even complain about paying $100,000 in taxes during 1939.

"It takes money to run a government and it takes money to relieve distress," he said when the check went off to the tax office. "As an American, I've always paid my way and I've always been glad to be able to pay my way. Those of us who make big dough are pretty lucky."

He was making more money than ever, although the $368,333 he had earned in the past twelve months was only the sixth highest total in the United States. Top of the list was now Gary Cooper, but Jimmy did not particularly care.

Not all of his money was coming from films. He was bigger than ever on radio, and although he did not want to make regular broadcasts, he could be guaranteed $5000 every time he went on the air. A Cagney radio show was always regarded as a big occasion.

He had appeared on shows with Alice Faye, Al Jolson, and all the others who had faithful audiences glued to their radios at regular hours every week. He had been on the Gertrude Lawrence program for Revlon and had twice been featured in what was always regarded as an important medium for film actors, the Lux Radio Theater. These featured broadcast adaptations of two of his film successes, *Ceiling Zero*—with his friend Ralph Bellamy in the O'Brien role—and with Pat O'Brien himself in *Angels with Dirty Faces*. Radio in 1940 provided big money, big audiences, and a tremendous public response.

Some of the radio casting in those days was surprising. In one play Cagney and Gracie Allen were featured in a story about the Dublin "Troubles" in 1916. Gracie, temporarily dropping her usual wacky stance for the dramatic role, portrayed Jimmy's sweetheart and eventual betrayer. According to *Variety,* it made a "brief but potent yarn." Since both were of Irish extraction, Cagney and Allen had sympathy for the idea being put forward. The paper said that Jimmy's own performance was "eloquently low-keyed and he ... handled the Irish brogue with apparent ease."

His most moving radio performance, however, came some months later in an adaptation of the Dalton Trumbo antiwar play *Johnny Got His Gun,* about a limbless veteran who wants to tell the world about the madness of war. Cagney declined to take a fee for doing it. "I did it for nothing," he explained, "because it was a brilliant argument against war." But the Radio Actors Guild stipulated that he could not do it for nothing. If he did, the Guild might lose everything it had won in the fight to keep amateurs off the air. So Jimmy agreed to take a fee after all—so long as it was not more than $33, the bare minimum negotiated by the Guild.

Jimmy's stance showed how disturbed he was by the turn of

world events. Europe was already at war and while, in international terms, he was a pacifist at heart, he did what he could to help the Allied cause. In June 1940 he joined Charles Laughton, Shirley Temple, and Paul Muni in a stage and radio show from Hollywood on behalf of the Red Cross European Relief Fund and helped raise $60,000. He also personally donated a fully equipped field ambulance to be sent to Europe.

"I believe," he said at the time, "that when war is declared and is an actual fact, we should do everything to relieve the distress of those who are its victims." It was, he explained in an interview with Ed Sullivan, no more than an extension of the feelings he had always had for the poor and underprivileged. "Our neighborhood was filled with decent, hard-working families who slaved all their lives and never got much out of it. So my sympathies have always been with the poor because that's where we came from—and I haven't forgotten it."

If the liberals in America cheered such sentiments, to others Jimmy's activities smacked of Communism. To them Cagney was still the Red they believed he had been in 1934. And now they had the backing of a congressional committee, which had decided to hold a full investigation.

The issue came to a head when John R. Leech, the former boss of the Communist Party in Los Angeles, appeared before the Los Angeles County grand jury. He handed them what he alleged to be a list of "heavy subscribers" to the party. The list, as he read it out, caused a sensation. The people he was accusing of being the backbone of the local party machine were all well known in Hollywood. As one name followed the other, the list grew more incredible: Jean Miller, actress; Clifford Odets, dramatist; Franchot Tone, Fredric March, Humphrey Bogart, Francis Lederer—and James Cagney, actors.

Leech said that some had bought "dues stamps" to bring their full membership of the party up to date. Among these was

Fredric March, who, he alleged, was a member of the party study group which was "purely organized by the Communist Party." As for Cagney, Leech said he had been both a member and a contributor. In a long and fairly plausible story, Leech agreed Jimmy had gone underground since 1935. But he said that had been on the advice of the party's head office which had been concerned at the "professional difficulties" experienced by Cagney following the unfavorable publicity at the time of the San Joaquin Valley cotton strike.

The story grew more elaborate as he told it: "Shortly thereafter, the Communist Party in New York notified the state committee which, in turn, notified me in writing that because of the unfavorable publicity, the California organization and particularly the Los Angeles organization must in the future have no contact with Mr. Cagney; that any relation between Mr. Cagney and the Communist Party would be considered entirely by the Central Committee of the Communist Party."

Most of the people named in Leech's statement were quick to brief their lawyers. Fredric March described Leech as an "unmitigated liar"—which, if untrue, could have been dangerous. But March was determined: "I will welcome the opportunity to meet Mr. Leech face to face and call him a liar," he said. "None of the charges of this man—who by his own admission is an ex-Communist and onetime advocate of our government's overthrow by force and violence—is true in the slightest degree. I do not even know the man."

Unfortunately, Jimmy was not able to react quite so quickly. He was motoring somewhere in New England without the car radio turned on and hadn't heard the charges. But his brother Bill did, and in his capacity as the Cagney business manager issued a statement: "I can speak for Jimmy in saying he is not a Communist, never has been a Communist, and never will be—because he is not in sympathy with the cause in any way and he has never contributed funds to the Communist Party." Bill repeated the well-known fact that his brother had contributed to help the cotton strikers get food and clothing for their wives and children. "But that was a humanitarian cause and Jimmy's contributions are always for deserving causes."

Four days later, Representative Martin Dies, who was known as a man with political ambitions, demanded that Cagney, March, and Franchot Tone appear before the House Un-American Activities Committee, of which he was now chairman. He said he "expected" they would comply and answer all the accusations being leveled.

Finally Jimmy was located at Chilmark, Massachusetts. He immediately denied that he had ever had anything to do with the Communist Party or was ever remotely a sympathizer. "You can blame it on West Coast political aspirants," he said angrily. The charges were "a lot of hooey" and he was flying to San Francisco to prove it. The fact that he was flying showed how worried and angry he was. He had never flown before, because of his pact with his wife Bill. But he knew he had to be in California as quickly as possible.

What were his politics? "Politically, I'm an American, a liberal Democrat," he told reporters at the airport on his arrival. "In the coming elections, I'm going to vote for President Roosevelt."

Cagney was being supported by William Wilson, a former commander of the American Ex-Servicemen's Association —and a more upright and acceptable organization could not be found. Dies himself, meanwhile, had reduced the extent of the charges he was making against Jimmy. He said the star was being investigated because he was thought to be "sympathetically inclined toward the Communists." It was less severe than the earlier accusation but still highly actionable, and Jimmy was determined to tell him so.

At the San Francisco inquiry, Cagney said that the allegations were "so exaggerated as to be ridiculous." So was Dies' latest charge: "Hollywood is permeated with Communism." Jimmy did not deny he had made contributions to a number of different organizations. But he said he did not consider any of them to be either Communist or un-American.

It did not take long for even Representative Dies to agree. After hearing Cagney's statements and listening to the other stars, he dismissed all the charges. Mr. Dies declared, as he did so: "Many actors, from humane motives, made contributions and let their names be used by certain organizations which the committee unanimously found to be organized under Communist leadership." He was determined to show that because there had been smoke, there could easily have been fire, too.

Ed Sullivan interviewed Jimmy for his New York *Daily News* feature "Little Old New York" and wondered why actors did not come out at the time that they made their donations and say they were made for humanitarian purposes without any strings attached. Why wait for allegations to be made at an official tribunal? Jimmy had to think about that, and then answered: "You feel peculiar about telling what a great humanitarian you are. My theory always has been that if you do something for someone less fortunate, do it and keep still about it."

"That theory didn't work out very well, did it?" asked Sullivan.

"I suppose not," Jimmy replied. "But I've taken about all that I'm going to take."

For most of the people who were content to be Cagney admirers from afar, the news of his being cleared by the Dies committee was more than welcome. It assured the continuation of their movie-going habits for the immediate future.

In *Each Dawn I Die,* which was playing in theaters at about the time the Dies "show" was playing in San Francisco, audiences saw Jimmy working with his usual passion. Ironically, it was the story of a wronged guy coming up against the forces of authority, only the character in the film was not as influential or lucky as Jimmy had been at the Dies hearing.

He played a muckraking reporter who discovers that the local district attorney is involved in a serious case of corruption, and so emblazons the story across the front page of his newspaper. The D.A. gets back by organizing a "bum rap" for the reporter in the form of a manslaughter charge. He is knocked out and then put in the cab of a crashed car, his body liberally sprinkled with alcohol.

As a result, he is sent to prison and there becomes as hard as the bread served at mealtimes. He gets friendly with another convict, played by George Raft, and helps organize for him an amazingly daring escape from the courtroom where an appeal is being heard. The escape seemed so perfect that years later it was to be blamed for a real-life flight. As the story progresses, Jimmy is double-crossed by Raft—to use the idiom of the film—and until the final reel everything goes hideously wrong. Everything, that is, except Cagney's acting. He fitted the role so beautifully that his jailhouse fatigues and striped cap looked as though they could have been designed originally for him.

Paul Holt in the London *Daily Express* entered into the full spirit of the film: "You know the way a gal wrinkles her nose at a guy when she means he can go ahead? Well, that's the way James Cagney wrinkles his nose when it meets the scent of something particularly sinister. . . . He gets his nose so near a hot piece that he gets it sunburned."

The picture was billed: "Killer meets Killer," which completely overlooked the fact that Cagney played a wronged, innocent man. All the publicity for the film was geared to exploiting the full potential of Cagney sizing up to Raft. One scene, in which the two come to blows wearing handcuffs, had to be shot four times. When it was all over, Jimmy felt so bruised that he told director William Keighley, "Remind me to check on my insurance."

Jimmy went to the farm when shooting stopped and stayed there while the critics and the first audiences were seeing the movie. "I've made so many prison pictures that I feel as though I've been let out on parole," he joked. It was also how he always felt when he left the Warner lot at the end of a fiming schedule. He said that Garbo had the right idea by already saying she wanted to be alone. "Though," he confessed, "I've never met her."

He had still not met half the names in Hollywood, partly because he and Bill did not like going to parties; partly because he was singularly unimpressed with people who just happened to have the looks and the lucky breaks that made them stars. If they reached stardom because of their acting abilities, that was another matter. He was always delighted to see an actor he admired at work—because it gave him an opportunity to learn. It was for that reason that he took Frank McHugh out for a drive soon after getting back to the West Coast.

They drove from Burbank to Warner Bros.' smaller Sunset studio in Hollywood, and there they just watched an old man on a set pick up a cup of coffee and say a few simple lines. The man was not well known. There was no likelihood of his ever becoming a star. But to Cagney he was an *Actor*.

When they left the studio, McHugh was still mystified.

But Jimmy was elated. Watching a true actor at work was the best way he knew of refreshing himself. And having been a gangster in thirteen pictures, been killed in eight of them, imprisoned in five, and socked his leading lady in four, he felt he needed that refreshment.

Not all the critics would have agreed. Howard Barnes said

in the New York *Herald Tribune:* "There are few screen actors who can touch James Cagney for that subtle combination of personality and artifice which constitutes motion picture make-believe. Moreover, in a particular field of melodrama, it seems to me he has no peers."

To prove Barnes correct, Warner Bros. put Jimmy back behind bars in his next film, *The Roaring Twenties,* a Prohibition story that could not have been more true to life had it been made in a still.

The film was pure Cagney, even with Humphrey Bogart in a subsidiary role and a vitally effective performance by Gladys George as a "speakeasy queen." It began in the trenches, and worthwhile use was made of newsreel film of boys returning from "over there." Cagney plays one of the returning heroes, who discovers that not only is his old job no longer open to him, but the girl he has been writing to throughout the war is still at school. He finds there is nothing for him to do to earn a crust but go outside the law. Paid to deliver a parcel of "meat," he discovers too late that it is really "laughing juice"—illegal liquor. Just as in all the previous pictures, the stretch in jail hardens him for the criminal life he has no alternative but to adopt.

Mark Hellinger wrote the story, which was originally called *The World Moves On.* In England, it was called *They Gave Him a Gun.* About ten years later, it was shown in the Soviet Union under the not-too-subtle title *The Fate of a Soldier in America.* Howard Barnes again jumped on to the Cagney wagon: "*The Roaring Twenties* would be little better than a sentimental and synthetic gangster melodrama were it not for James Cagney's contribution to the show."

Warner Bros. put him back in uniform in his very next picture, *The Fighting 69th.* It turned out to be as much Pat O'Brien's film as Cagney's—with O'Brien playing the legendary soldier-priest Father Duffy, it could hardly be expected to be otherwise. Jimmy, with an Army gun in his hand, and "Paddy," with a Bible in his, were examples of inspired casting.

The Fighting 69th was an actual New York Irish regiment in World War I. With New York full of Irishmen, and Cagney and O'Brien frequently regarded as their uncanonized patron saints, Warner Bros. spared nothing to put *The Fighting 69th* before the public. The Army approved the film—because it might get more men attuned to the possibilities of fighting a war. Jack Warner's idea was more commercial. To show that the studio pulled no punches in its patriotism, he hired the *Twentieth Century Ltd.* and brought the film's cast from California to New York for the picture's premiere—all the cast, that is, except Jimmy. He had been resting at Martha's Vineyard. But how could he be left out of a shindig like this? The publicity machine, as always, had the answer.

For the first time in its known history, the express train broke its journey just before it reached its final destination. At the 125th Street Station, Jimmy was waiting as the train stopped. He got aboard and was immediately escorted to the private drawing room occupied by Pat O'Brien and his old adversary Jack Warner. When the train reached Grand Central Station a few minutes later, Jimmy was the first to get off, and he led a parade out into the street. While the band of the 165th Regiment played "Hail, Hail, the Gang's All Here," Jimmy and the rest of the Warner Bros. party had to fight their way through some ten thousand fans. *The Fighting 69th* was the usual Cagney-O'Brien blockbuster, and the publicity-department chiefs each got a bonus. The stunt could only have been successful in those days, when a crowd offered no more threat than the possibility of someone's losing an autograph book.

In the film Jimmy played the braggart who turns yellow in the trenches, just as he played the tough guy in *Angels with*

Dirty Faces. He walked as if his heels were still on foam rubber, and his index finger jabbed in the way it did in Chicago or New York's East Side. The public liked the Cagney-O'Brien partnership, and also liked the amalgam of the pair with Ann Sheridan.

Next Warner Bros. put the three in a film called *Torrid Zone,* which really should never have been made. It was a poor film and Cagney's performance was really mediocre. But the New York *World Telegram* said Jimmy managed to "express a complete characterization with one little gesture."

In 1941 he started work on a film called *City for Conquest,* about a prize fighter who becomes a victim of big business. It could easily have been the familiar corny story about the boxer who is blinded and the kid brother who wants to write a symphony, but Cagney would not play a blind man selling newspapers on the streets of New York, so he did the only thing that seemed possible to him: he went to the street and found himself a blind newspaper seller. For days, he watched the man at work, saw him organizing his newspapers, and studied how he made change. What fascinated him particularly was the way the blind man would talk to a customer, thinking he was looking him straight in the face, yet the gaze of his sightless eyes was inevitably directed far from the right point. It took Jimmy days to perfect that gesture.

His scenes in the boxing ring were equally well rehearsed. He used no extras, and he fought as though he were once more seeking the bantamweight title in Yorkville. His opponent, a youngster called Joey Gray, was not always as careful to avoid actual punches as Jimmy was to miss him. Cagney had been especially equipped with a set of rubber teeth guards, but Gray aimed one blow that hit him "straight in the chops." The teeth guard was dislodged, and Jimmy was momentarily stunned. He decided to give the younger man something to remember, and his next punch did not miss either. "You all right, Joey?" he asked afterward.

Gray replied, "I saw my whole family!"

Even when Cagney was not making a fight film, there would frequently be a boxing ring off the set in which he could spar and help keep the pounds away. He also liked to talk about some of the things that happened in movies when two actors were supposed to hit each other. One of his favorite anecdotes is about the confrontation that occurred at about the same time as *City for Conquest* was being made—between his old friend Allen Jenkins and Errol Flynn, who was said to have "muscles behind his ears." The director, Michael Curtiz, tried to persuade Jenkins to stop ducking every time Flynn swung in his direction.

"Allen, Allen," he cried. "He wouldn't hurt you. Don't pull back."

But it happened again, and Curtiz again tried to persuade him to keep his chin up.

"All right," said Jenkins. "I won't duck. I'll try again—but if Flynn hits me, I'll break your goddamn nose."

"Print the last one," yelled Curtiz.

Once all the production work was over, the way *City for Conquest* was finally edited made Cagney vow never again to see one of his films. He explained why, years afterward: "I trained as though I were going into a ten-rounder. And then I saw it cut. I said: 'What for, what for, what for?' The editing took an awful lot of the sound, solid substance out of it."

Just the same, *City for Conquest* undoubtedly did work and Cagney recognizes it now as one of his favorite films. The film also worked in another, unexpected way. *The New York Times,* after praising the work of Cagney and his female lead Ann

Sheridan, added: "Best of the supporting players is Elia Kazan, a Group Theatre boy who does a gangster that would scare Eddie Robinson."

Kazan, who was to become one of Hollywood's most celebrated directors, acknowledged the effect that working with Cagney in *City for Conquest* had had on his own career: "I learned something from Jimmy Cagney—he taught me quite a lot about acting. Jimmy taught me some things about being honest and not overdoing it. He even affected my work with Brando a little bit. I mean, 'Don't show it. Just do it.' "

The *Sunday Express* in London was equally admiring of the Cagney performance: "If you saw Jimmy Cagney in *City for Conquest,*" they wrote early in 1941, "you will notice a violent change in the star's makeup, requiring the hard-boiled star to be softly cooked for three minutes. I'm certain Jimmy enjoyed this picture in which his cynical, smirky, you're-telling-me stuff was transformed into the sentiment of a real human being."

Nearer home, the *Morning Telegraph*'s judgment on *City for Conquest* was to heap its praise on Cagney and Ann Sheridan, whose "personalities are more than enough to make up for the deficiencies of *City for Conquest,* and whatever success the picture enjoys—which should be considerable—may be laid to the presence of these two stars in the cast, rather than to any ingenuity in plot, characterization, or development."

In his next film, *The Strawberry Blonde,* Cagney played a different character altogether—a dentist with a derby hat tipped over one eye the way his father would wear one after too much drinking. He is a dentist who was always happier at a fairground than in his office, and his instruments look as though they would have been better suited to a carpenter. He loses the strawberry blonde in question (Rita Hayworth) to con man Jack Carson, who allows Jimmy to go to jail for his own corruption. All the five years that he is in prison, he has waiting for him a kind, gentle wife played by Olivia de Havilland. There were beautiful performances all around and a charming comic twist at the film's end. Carson goes to have a tooth pulled and Cagney plans to use a fatal dose of gas. But he thinks better of it—and in the end, pulls the tooth with no anesthetic at all.

Jimmy was rightly happy with *The Strawberry Blonde.* He was also happier with his own life than he had been for a very long time. He and Bill had just adopted two children—a boy they called James Cagney, Jr., and a girl named Casey. When Jimmy was not playing the family man, he was driving tractors, sowing crops, and learning more about the animals on the farm.

But probably neither Jimmy nor Bill was as happy as the new Cagney children's grandmother. Carrie still lived with her younger doctor son Ed and at sixty-three was still a red-headed Irishwoman as stubborn as any legend might make her. Both Jimmy and her son Bill begged her to move from the business district to Beverly Hills, where they both had homes, but she said she wanted to stay put. She saw her boys and their families whenever she wanted to and saw no reason to move to an address that might seem more smart than where she now lived.

Family ties were still very close. Whenever Harry left Queens for a vacation on the Coast, all the brothers invariably would get together for an impromptu singing quartet, with Jimmy providing the musical backing on the guitar. Outsiders sometimes saw in the Cagney clan the making of a society even more secret than the "Irish Mafia," and the brothers did not deny it. They all agreed they were mulishly stubborn. As Bill said about his brothers and himself: "We love everybody—and don't give a damn for anybody."

The studio next had Jimmy opposite Bette Davis in a picture called *The Bride Came C.O.D.* It was about a broadcaster (Cagney) chartering his private plane to a couple of elopers (Miss Davis and Jack Carson). In true blackguard fashion,

Jimmy promises to deliver the runaway bride to her father and collect the reward, C.O.D. The plane crashes and Jimmy spends the night sleeping on the desert sands where it force-landed. The New York *Post* summed it up: "Okay, Jimmy and Bette. You've had your fling. Now go back to work."

When Jimmy did go back to work, it was to play a pilot again—but a different kind of pilot in an altogether different kind of film. For one thing, it was his first in color. For another, *Captains of the Clouds* was a patriotic vehicle at a time when the Japanese were planning their assault on Pearl Harbor. Because America was still out of the war herself, Jimmy plays a pilot in the Royal Canadian Air Force. The aerial dogfights were exciting cinema, and so were Cagney's performance and Michael Curtiz's direction. To the New York *Post* it represented a "pure tribute to the unchanging forcefulness of James Cagney."

Two hundred Canadian Air Force cadets came to New York for the film's opening, each of them matched with a glamorous model provided by the studio. By the time the movie was released, the patriotic spirit had caught the whole country. America was at war and the studios started work earlier in the morning so that they could have everything finished in time for the evening blackout. Before the end of 1941, Jimmy's stand-in had already joined the Navy and taken with him his wardrobe man and his secretary.

Jimmy would have liked to volunteer himself, but the services had not yet gotten around to taking forty-two-year-olds. Instead, Warner Bros. advised him to go and see an old film called *The Phantom President*.

14 YANKEE DOODLE DANDY

THE NEW proposition offered Jimmy by Warner Bros. seemed to guarantee everything he could want: a moving story about a forceful character, and a part in which he could act his head off, sing all he wanted to, and dance enough to make the leading hoofers in Hollywood jealous. The money would be all right, too.

Others mentioned that the part could give him the chance to do something which, in later years, would be regarded as a memorial to his art. That was a notion he scorned. He still did not think his status in the world of show business deserved any such accolade. The studio was just the place he went early in the morning after feeding the ducks and chickens. Keeping those birds was part of his war effort, and to him it seemed more important work than making films.

But something about this Warner Bros. idea was more than tempting. In fact, Jimmy and his brother Bill had talked over the very same suggestion more than a year before. When people were still talking about the Dies hearings, Bill had gone to Jack Warner and told him: "There's just one thing to do. We should make a movie with Jimmy playing the damnedest patriotic man in the country." When Warner asked him who he had in mind, Bill replied: "George M. Cohan."

Now Warner had come around to the same way of thinking. It would be a good story, and this was undoubtedly the time to make it. Cohan was the Irish-American who unashamedly draped a flag around himself in almost every show he put on Broadway. He was once asked if he could write a show without a flag in it and his answer has gone down into folklore: "I can write without anything but a pencil." He wrote "Yankee Doodle Boy" and "You're a Grand Old Flag" and a song the studio thought would do the country good to hear again, "Over There."

In fact, Cohan had written some five hundred songs and was the admitted inspiration of Irving Berlin and a score of other song writers. He had also made an impressive impact performing in straight plays by other people, like Eugene O'Neill's *Ah, Wilderness!*

Jimmy had to agree that the idea, if acted upon, could represent a career milestone. He had long since forgiven Cohan for not recognizing his talent at that long-ago audition. In the late thirties, he and his wife Bill had watched Cohan playing President Roosevelt in *I'd Rather Be Right* by Rodgers and Hart. When the curtain came down, they had clapped themselves sore. Now, at Jack Warner's suggestion, Jimmy had seen an even earlier Cohan venture, the rickety *Phantom President.* He had watched Cohan walking and talking in the film and decided that yes, he could interpret George M. on the screen. But first there would be problems to iron out.

Cohan was not nearly so modest about his place in the world of entertainment as was Cagney. At about the same time he was playing in *I'd Rather Be Right,* he had been talking about his eventual life over dinner with George Jessel. Jessel believed he knew more about show business than anyone else living and, despite his eccentricities, it remains a fair judgment today.

In the early hours of a summer morning, Cohan mused to Jessel about his idea for a musical play in which for the first time in his almost fifty-year-long career he would be interpolating songs from his other shows. There would also be a series of flashbacks to the old plays. Jessel said he thought the idea was great—but it would be much better as a film, a picture that would also tell the Cohan story for the first time.

"Maybe, it would, kid," Cohan said to Jessel. "But I'm not looking forward to any association with those guys out there."

"Those guys out there" were the Hollywood moguls who did not rate particularly high on Cohan's show-business totem pole. Jessel said later that Cohan felt he had been "treated in about the same manner as Dreyfus was at Devil's Island." But Jessel, who was now a film producer, had his agent Jack Curtis talk it over with Cohan's West Coast lawyer. Soon they got a deal moving with MGM. They even decided on a title: *The Four Cohans,* based on the act George M. had had with his father, mother, and sister before making it big on his own. The idea died, because George M. insisted on the right to edit the manuscript and effectively have the last word. And at MGM, only Louis B. Mayer ever had the last word.

But by this time, Cohan had already assembled a great many notes and had written the bulk of his own screenplay. He even talked about playing his own father—just so he could be constantly around. The main role of himself would go, they agreed, to Mickey Rooney.

The big problem was that MGM was not alone in its reluctance to give a final say to Cohan. He had a reputation for being difficult in everything he touched. In 1919 he had joined the producers against the actors when Broadway experienced its first strike. His rows with others in the business made James Cagney's relationship with Warner Bros. seem like a lovers' tiff. But finally, long after Jessel had drifted from the scene, the Cagney idea was put to a now aging and sick George M. Cohan. A deal was struck. Cohan would get the memorial he certainly did crave—he had not yet thought about the statue which would go up on Broadway after his death—and a check for $100,000. He would allow any one of his five hundred songs to be used in the picture, and he would also have the right to veto the script.

He agreed, too, that Jimmy would play the main part and that his brother Bill would, for the first time, be cast as producer. Jack Warner was delighted, but he offered the Cagneys one sentence of warning: "Just don't mess around with that script once Cohan has approved it." They listened to the warning and then decided to completely ignore it.

First the two Cagneys agreed to reject the idea of calling the picture *The Four Cohans.* They turned down, too, *The George M. Cohan Story*—George M. was enough of a realist to accept that it could never quite be that. Instead, the brothers decided to take part of the chorus of Cohan's famous song "Yankee Doodle Boy" and call the film *Yankee Doodle Dandy.*

For days, they went over the original script, wrestled with the problems they considered it presented, and then agreed they had no alternative but to get a new one. But before they did so, they had to decide on what sort of performance Jimmy was aiming for. Was he going to become a carbon-copy Cohan or would he be more his own man? He decided he was going to be James Cagney playing George M. Cohan as he saw him. He would not aim at impersonating him. Jimmy remembered the story about Cohan going up to a man who had just impersonated him on the stage, and telling him: "Son, one of us is awful bad." So he agreed that he would try to present his own view of both Cohan the performer and Cohan the man.

Jimmy saw as many clips as he could obtain of George M. at work and tried to find a way of presenting him without making it look like an impersonation. The Cagney pose with the pointed index finger was remarkably similar to the way Cohan would point for effect with arm outstretched in the middle of a song. His own tiptoe walk was not exactly the same India-rubber stance that Cohan adopted, but Jimmy found a way of making the two poses combine into a puppetlike movement. He discovered he could dance while making his legs look as though they belonged to someone else.

Cohan off stage had to be, he decided, a portrait and not a caricature. He would not walk the way he did on stage. He would not talk as though he were in the middle of a song. This decision in itself was a novel departure from the usual practice of showing an entertainer behaving at home exactly as he did on stage. When he finally got to Cohan's late years, he agreed to adopt a hoarse sound to his voice—and one which since then has been copied by Cagney impersonators almost as frequently as they have adopted his portrait of the Yorkville pimp.

But before any of these plans could be put into operation, the question of the script had to be ironed out. They clearly thought the original screenplay did not do the story justice. But before they had settled on an alternative, Jack Warner entered the picture again and insisted that shooting had to begin.

Warner could see no reason why it should not. He had a complete cast already to go before the cameras. Joan Leslie was signed to play Cohan's wife. Rosemary de Camp was going to be his mother and for Cohan's father, there was the inspired choice of Walter Huston—for whom Cohan had written his play *Elmer the Great,* based on a Ring Lardner story.

And then there was the pretty girl who had been contracted to play Cohan's younger sister. She was Jimmy's own young sister, Jeanne. In the end, it was Jeanne who was to ensure that *Yankee Doodle Dandy* actually got beyond the talking stage.

The day before shooting was planned to start, Jimmy had made up his mind not to go through with it. He did not think he could do anything with the part as it was laid down in the screenplay. Sitting on the tailboard of a truck in the Burbank grounds, he told his brother he could not make anything of the role and as a result there could not be a good film. If he left the set of *Yankee Doodle Dandy*—and he was determined to do so—he wouldn't come back to make any other pictures. He was leaving and taking Bill and the children off to the farm.

It was then that Jeanne joined her two brothers. Jimmy saw the excitement on her face at the prospect of working on the picture, and Bill saw it too. Instantly, the two brothers agreed they had to make a go of it—if only not to let Jeanne down. Whatever they felt themselves, they were not going to spoil her big chance. It was to prove to be the most sensible decision Jimmy had made since accepting Darryl Zanuck's offer of a railroad ticket thirteen years before.

But now they had to get the question of the screenplay settled. It was done that same day. Twenty-four hours later, shooting was due to begin, but now at that late notice, three new writers were brought in and told what was needed: almost the Cohan story, but not quite. Director Michael Curtiz approved of the changes and the Epstein brothers, Julius and Philip, together with Edmund Joseph, agreed to provide a new script.

The important thing was to be the Cohan songs and the Cohan performances. It also had to be both patriotic and a warm family story. And if it was not going to be entirely lost on audiences that Cohan could be a bit of a rogue, Cagney made him a lovable rogue. The writers did not bother with the actors' strike. No one complained that the rough Irish knockabout humor indulged in by the Four Cohans in their act looked a lot more restrained on the screen. Both Cohans—Senior and Junior—were more attractive in the tailcoats they wore in the film than in the country-bumpkin clothes they actually wore on stage. Cohan's famous curtain speech—"My mother thanks you, my father thanks you, my sister thanks you, and I thank you"—sounded perfect coming from Cagney.

Liberties were taken throughout with the true Cohan story. Cohan used to like to say that he was born on the Fourth of July. He was not; he was born on the third. But using the true date in the film would have spoiled the story that he always thought the flags flying that day were in honor of his birthday. It might also have ruined the effect of the line in "Yankee Doodle Boy" which actually stated that he was "born on the Fourth of July." So Fourth of July it was in the film, too.

Then there was the meeting with President Roosevelt. The picture began with Cohan being summoned to the White House from the stage door of the Washington, D.C., theater where he was playing in *I'd Rather Be Right*. He is welcomed to the mansion by a black footman who reveals he has always been a Cohan fan. Inside the Oval Office, Roosevelt (Captain Jack Young giving the first film impersonation of a living president) invites the entertainer to sit down. Cohan believes he is going to be chastised for *I'd Rather Be Right*. Instead, the president asks him how he got started in show business. From there on, the story flashes back to his birth in Rhode Island—on the Fourth of July—and goes on through the events of his life, with the occasional sound commentary reminding the audience that the president is still listening. At the picture's end, the Chief Executive hands Cohan the Congressional Medal of Honor.

It was all very touching and very believable—especially as on his way home through the rain-swept streets, Cohan is chided by a soldier for not joining in the song being played by a military band. It is, of course, "Over There." None of it ever happened.

I'd Rather Be Right played in 1939, and the Congressional Medal of Honor was awarded in 1936. Today, it stands in a place of honor, in a glass case, at the New York Lambs Club.

What was believable for everybody working on the movie was the rapport between Jimmy and Jeanne. Perhaps partly because of her great influence in getting the picture off the ground, but mostly because of their mutual affection for each other, Jimmy was constantly watching over her, helping her with her lines, and generally making her feel comfortable.

"You've no idea what it is like, what a wonderful feeling it is to look across the set while playing a scene and seeing Jimmy there," she said at the time. "It's a great help." She could see how Jimmy planned his work, how he deliberately put extra emphasis on the dramatic moments so as not to get stale while concentrating on the musical numbers. The relationship between brother and sister was touching to witness.

The most touching moment of all, though, was when Cohan, at the bedside of his dying father, had to tell him about the show he had just left. Yes, he lied, he had recited the familiar curtain speech. Then, with choking voice, he repeats it for the old man. Hardbitten newspapermen wept unashamedly when they first saw it, and still do. When the scene was being shot, tears streaked down the faces of the people on the studio floor—among them Michael Curtiz, the director. "Gott, Jeemy," he said, "that was marvelous"—and went off to find a clean handkerchief.

The Cagneys felt sure Cohan would accept all the story's "white lies" as well as the sentiment. But there was a problem which might not be so easily sorted out. How, they wondered, would he take to his wife being called Mary? He had been married twice, once to the English actress Ethel Levey, the second time to the woman who was still his wife—and she was called Agnes. Since the story only gave him one wife, the writers suggested calling her by the name of one of Cohan's most important songs, "Mary."

On one point, the *Yankee Doodle* team did not breach any faith with Cohan. He had stipulated "no love scenes," and Jimmy did not once kiss Joan Leslie. Not that he really had to. When he sang "Mary" to her, it was one of the best love scenes the cinema had ever known.

But there were a few moments in the picture that had actually happened. One of these was when Cohan meets Eddie Foy. Foy, head of another celebrated Broadway family—Eddie Foy and the Seven Little Foys—gazes at a billboard advertising a new show starring George M. Cohan, produced by George M. Cohan. Beautifully playing his own father, Eddie Foy, Jr., curls up his lips in typical Foy fashion and tells the man standing next to him—Cohan, of course—that he had never heard of any of the people on the advertisement. The only diversion from reality was that in the movie it all looked very amusing and pleasant. In fact, Foy and Cohan hated each other.

Irving Berlin says *Yankee Doodle Dandy* is the one movie made of a song writer's life that does not actually make him squirm. The one reason he will never allow his own story to be told on film is simply that no one could guarantee it would turn out like the Cohan picture. But before its release in 1942, no one knew what the public would make of it. Worst of all, no one at Warner Bros. knew what George M. would make of it.

The film had cost $1.5 million, even though it was made in black and white. (It is all those flags that make so many people think it was in color, says Cagney.) Jack L. Warner had previously discovered what the Cagneys had done to the original screenplay, but he agreed to play along with them because shooting had gone beyond the point of no return. Now he was petrified about what Cohan might say. The choice was either receiving Cohan's blessing or throwing the whole lot on the scrap heap.

Warner spent days rehearsing the speech he was going to make to Cohan. He did not need it. Cohan had found out by certain unexplained but devious means about what had happened and phoned "the guys out there" to find out more. For the moment, the matter was put in the hands of his West Coast representative, Edward Raftery, then president of United Artists. It was a fortunate choice of go-between—because Bill Cagney had been talking about pulling his brother away from Warner Bros. and setting up their own operation. United Artists would handle distribution. With that thought in mind, Bill persuaded Raftery to wait until a rough cut of the picture was available before entering into any negotiation on Cohan's behalf. When the cut was finally ready and Raftery saw it, he told Bill Cagney: "I'd say you're all right."

But he could not be sure. For one thing, Cohan himself was not sure either. He saw the film at a private showing in New York and when the lights went on refused to give the men from Warner Bros. who were with him an instant answer. All he would say was he would have to see what his wife Agnes thought.

Agnes had not been able to see the film with her husband. She was ill in a hospital in upstate New York, and George M. would not commit himself until he had gauged her reaction to being portrayed by Joan Leslie and called Mary. Mrs. Cohan saw the film sitting in a small disused fire station. There was no movie house in the town where her hospital was situated, and portable projection equipment was set up in the nearest available hall.

Nobody spoke during the showing. When the movie was over, the Warner Bros. men who had come along with the equipment looked at George M. and saw that he was looking at Agnes. It seemed that an enormous row was now inevitable. Cohan spoke first. "About that Mary business . . ." he said, still looking at his wife. But Agnes reached out for her husband and threw her arms around his neck. "I always knew you had me in mind when you wrote that song," she said. "Thank you." She then gave him precisely the sort of kiss he had ordered kept out of the picture.

The very next moment, Cohan dictated a telegram to Cagney thanking him for a new life in his old age. There were sighs of relief all round, not least of them from Jimmy himself. He had completed the greatest performance of his life. And he had done it without a gun, a punch, or a grapefruit. Yet as Cohan he was the same brand of pugnacious Irishman he had been all along. It was, nevertheless, his supreme triumph. He had proved he could be accepted as a song-and-dance man. For years he had been singing, but usually only in the bath or on the farm. When he did it on the stage or in his films, his brother Bill was not always the only one to duck from embarrassment. But now he sang in his peculiar amalgam of Cagney and Cohan, and had found a new voice.

Cagney agrees it was his most satisfying picture, the one of which he is most proud. As he told me himself: "I had the objective approach to do what I thought was required. You get as close to the man as possible without actually trying to become him—which I think is one of the fallacies today in the mind of the young actors. They try to *become* the characters they are playing. Therefore, if they do, they have no perspective on it. You have to stand back and take a good look at what you are doing."

But there was another reason why his performance was so effective. "Cohan was a song-and-dance man, which I had been from the very start," said Cagney. "So I understood the type. He was Irish and I was Irish, so there was no great decision to make. We just did it."

As a result of "just doing it," Jimmy won his first and only Academy Award. But it is not the Oscar that excites him about the film. He is much more gratified about the way the film was put together. "It had comedy in it. It had singing and dancing in it, and it had some drama. I always say this: Mr. Cohan gave us fifty years of a very troubled life and we just put his life to music. And that just about covers it."

The film was Cagney's triumph, but Cohan liked to foster the idea that it was his picture. An unusual insight into the way Cohan saw himself came in a piece of nonsense he wrote that was published in *The New York Times*. It was called "A Dandy Doodling Yankee."

Cohan imagined two old vaudeville veterans meeting on Broadway and discussing the new picture. One was called Frisby, the other Doaks, and he allowed himself an occasional barb at "the guys out there" in this conversation about the author of the piece:

DOAKS: Say, whatever became of that guy?
FRISBY: Cohan?
DOAKS: Yeah.
FRISBY: They say he's resting on his laurels.
DOAKS: On his what?
FRISBY: Never mind. Let it go.
DOAKS: What's laurels mean?
FRISBY: It means he ain't working.

DOAKS:	Looks like it. This guy Cagney's playing his part.
FRISBY:	Yeah? What's the play?
DOAKS:	T'ain't a play. It's a picture—a movin' picture. Called *Yankee Doodle Dandy*.
FRISBY:	Why didn't he play himself?
DOAKS:	I guess they didn't want him....
DOAKS:	Well, you say he didn't write the picture and he ain't in the picture. Then, where does the picture get off to be all about him?
FRISBY:	It ain't about him! It's about the things he's done....
DOAKS:	What did you think of it?
FRISBY:	This guy Cagney's great.
DOAKS:	Never mind about Cagney. How's the picture?
FRISBY:	Well, wait till you see it.

When the film opened in Los Angeles, it was decided that tickets would not cost a cent—provided the people attending bought war bonds instead. In Hollywood, the first bond was bought by Al Jolson for $25,000. He said it had been money well spent, and secretly hoped that someone would make a film like that about his own life. (His wish was to be granted. Four years later, *The Jolson Story* gave him an entirely new career.)

In New York, it was decided that the best seats at the Hollywood Theater would also go for a $25,000 war-bond donation. The first person to buy a bond at the box office was former governor Al Smith. The amount he spent was not disclosed. Another one in the line was Mrs. V. K. Wellington Koo, wife of the Chinese ambassador to London, who paid $1000. Other bonds on sale were priced at $12,500, $10,000, $5000, $1000, $500, $100, $50 and $25. Mrs. Douglas Gibbons, who was heading the committee in charge of ticket sales, revealed that she was hoping $5 million would be raised. Sales on the first night actually totaled $5 million—enough to buy three Liberty cargo vessels under construction and needed for the Atlantic convoy run. It was announced that the names of all donors would be engraved on panels installed in the captain's cabin of every ship.

So many people were milling around the theater on opening night that soldiers had to help control the crowds. Then, in the true spirit of the occasion, just before the curtain went up, an announcer gave away spare tickets—paid for in bond donations by people who could not attend—to some of the troops. Cohan, the patriot, said he approved heartily.

On the Fourth of July, 1942, Mayor Fiorello La Guardia proclaimed "George M. Cohan Day." The following November, after extensive intestinal surgery, George M. died. President Roosevelt was among those who sent his condolences. But Cohan had just seen one of the biggest show-biz successes of his or anyone else's life.

Bosley Crowther, writing in *The New York Times,* declared: "*Yankee Doodle Dandy* rode into town last night on a whole lot more than a pony. It rode on a star-spangled crest of one of the fanciest buildups that Broadway has ever known." He said it gave an "abundance of pleasure," and he added: "Everyone connected with it can stick a feather in his hat, and take our word—it's a dandy."

In the Sunday edition of the paper, he embroidered on his enthusiasm. "The truly remarkable nature of Mr. Cagney's accomplishment turns not so much on a literal imitation of Mr. Cohan as it does on a shrewd and meticulous creation of a lusty, spontaneous character."

To the *Motion Picture Herald,* it was a "wartimely inspiration." The *Herald Tribune*'s Howard Barnes called the film a "captivating record of a whole epoch." The story, he said, was "welded into beguiling continuity." As for Cagney, Barnes said: "He adds his own individual reflection to the part as should certainly be done in any dramatic impersonation of a celebrated figure. He has given many memorable and varied performances in the past, but this is nothing short of a brilliant tour-de-force of make believe."

The film was given an equally enthusiastic welcome in London. There, too, tickets went in exchange for contributions to war services, with certificates and bonds going for between £5 and £5,000 each. The scheme was given the blessing of Chancellor of the Exchequer Sir Kingsley Wood, and a total of £870,269 was raised at the premiere.

The British press was as enthusiastic as were the American writers. The *Daily Mirror* said: "Just seen a great new musical comedy star. In its way, it's the biggest discovery of the war. The name? James Cagney. Yes, I mean it. In *Yankee Doodle Dandy*, this lady-socking tough guy dances and sings like Fred Astaire and puts up his best acting performance to date."

To the *Evening Standard,* the picture represented "a sumptuous, bumptious, brilliant study." But the *Daily Worker* saw it as a good opportunity to wonder why Cagney had been so embarrassed by the old Communism charge as to want to prove his patriotism by making the film. "No doubt James Cagney is no Communist," said the paper. "But he was not afraid to show himself a good anti-fascist long before many other big shots of the cinema found the line opportune.... Furthermore, how does acting the part of a patriotic citizen prove a man is not a Communist? And where does that put the fighting men of the Red Army, for example?"

C. A. Lejeune of *The Observer,* one of Britain's most distinguished critics, announced that she considered James Cagney to be "my best actor." She compared him with Spencer Tracy, "who is a good player, one of my special favorites, but he can go blunderingly wrong at times. Cagney has never gone wrong in any part from musical comedy to Shakespeare's Bottom. Films have let Cagney down, but in thirteen years, I have never known Cagney to let down a picture."

Warner Bros. themselves described the film as their "most distinguished contribution to the American screen." Jimmy's was not the only Oscar nomination; there were eight others. Ray Heindorf and Heinz Roemehld won awards for the best scoring of a musical; Nathan Levinson received another for the sound track.

The evening the presentations were made had gone down as one of the most notable and also one of the most embarrassing in the history of the Oscar. Losing actresses wept copiously and were seen to push other stars sitting with them in the body of the hall. The speeches were the most boring anyone could remember until Irving Berlin came on to pay tribute to Cohan and Jimmy himself appeared.

After acknowledging the introduction from Gary Cooper, Cagney put the whole ceremony into his own idea of perspective. "I've always maintained," he said, "that in this business you are only as good as the other fellow thinks you are. It's nice to know that you people thought I had done a good job. And don't forget that it was a good part, too. Thank you very much."

With that, he hugged Greer Garson, who had just won her Oscar for *Mrs. Miniver,* and sat down while the crowd cheered. Those listening to the ceremony thought it was one of Cagney's best performances. It was certainly the best speech ever heard at an Oscar ceremony.

15 THE GALLANT HOURS

THE SUCCESS of *Yankee Doodle Dandy* might have led most people to think that Jimmy and Warner Bros. would stay with each other, but that was not how either Cagney brother saw it. Before anyone could have known just how much of a financial triumph they had on their hands, Jimmy and Bill thumbed their noses at the Burbank studio.

Now they were really going it alone, and Jimmy was signing no more long-term contracts with any studio. He was doing what almost every other top star would do twenty years later. But in August 1942, when Bill announced he was setting up William Cagney Productions, Inc., the whole industry was shocked. Bill, the inoffensive-looking monster of a deal-maker, was going to be president of the new company. His brother would be his deputy and principal actor.

Public reaction was the same as when United Artists had been set up by Douglas Fairbanks, Mary Pickford, and Charlie Chaplin: "The lunatics have taken over the asylum."

If Hollywood was an asylum, Jimmy's madness had become an extremely profitable one. In 1941, he had earned $362,500, which beat Clark Gable's salary by $5000. The figures, released by the Securities and Exchange Commission, also revealed that Bette Davis had earned $271,083, while Warner Bros.' production chief Hal Wallis had earned a mere $260,000.

Jimmy did not now need the additional money independent production could possibly earn him. Nor did he need to prove anything to Jack Warner. The appeal of the new company was that finally he would be his own boss.

The new arrangement did not stop Jimmy from continuing to enjoy the praise being heaped on him for his last Warner Bros. project. *The Sign,* the national Catholic monthly, named *Yankee Doodle Dandy* the recipient of its first award for motion picture of the year. More importantly, *The New York Times* had it on its list of 1942's ten best films. Cagney himself was voted by the *Times* the best male performer of the year. At New York's Hotel Berkshire, the city's critics presented him with a special award for the film, and extracts from *Yankee Doodle* were broadcast over the "Blue Network." When the Screen Guild put their play of the year over WABC they chose *Yankee Doodle Dandy* starring James Cagney. The list of honors went on and on.

Jeanne was in demand after her role in the picture, too. She proudly went back to New York, heading the class of '38 in the Hunter College Alumnae Association's Thanksgiving Day ceremonies. She told her audience: "The best thing that college students can do to help the war is what they are doing now—preparing themselves to be a constructive force in the postwar world."

Jimmy was happy to give his approval to such sentiments. He had a great interest in young people and when they sent him fan mail, these were the letters he appreciated most of all.

None was more appreciated than the note from a seventeen-year-old English girl in a hospital's plastic surgery ward. A few days later, she was able to open a large envelope with her bandaged hands. Inside was a picture bearing the message: "To Joan Hayes. Best o'luck—from your friend Jim Cagney."

He had first heard about her from his friend and fellow film actor Robert Montgomery when he visited the hospital where she was receiving treatment. He found she had been dug up out of the wreckage of the bombed London candy factory where she had been working. During the raid she had been covered with boiling glucose.

Jimmy was so moved by the story that he began corresponding with her. In addition to the photograph, he wrote: "Dear Joan. I just heard from Bob Montgomery that you are well on the mend." She was so thrilled by this gesture that she really did start on the mend. Jimmy was showing the same compassion he had shown during the troubles of the San Joaquin cotton pickers—only this time no one said anything about his being a Communist.

Next Jimmy applied his efforts to getting a better deal for less successful film actors and actresses. The star who had for many years been something of a one-man union now took on the job officially, succeeding Edward Arnold as president of the Screen Actors Guild by acclamation. It was the most unusual trade union in the world, but its members—partly because of the pulling power and near-blackmail possibilities offered by their names—took its work very seriously. Cary Grant was first vice-president and the list of the names of other directors of the Guild included George Murphy—who one day was to become a United States senator—Walter Pidgeon, Franchot Tone, and Jane Wyman.

One of the aims of the Guild was to improve the working conditions of its members. Now, as vice-president of William

Cagney Productions, Jimmy felt he had the best conditions in which to work in his entire career. The first film they were making was to be called *Johnny Come Lately,* and they had a promise from United Artists to handle the distribution. Considering both organizations' origins, it was a link of kindred spirits.

Johnny Come Lately was the story of a newspaper owner caught up in a scandal. Grace George starred with Cagney as the elderly newspaper owner who takes him under her wing when he is released from jail on parole. Also in the picture were other respected Hollywood names like Marjorie Main and Hattie McDaniel.

It was totally different from *Yankee Doodle Dandy.* In fact, Bill Cagney said his brother had chosen *Johnny Come Lately* simply because it "doesn't try to compete with the drama in the newspapers and isn't a big, spectacular job. It's just a story about a hobo and an old lady with plenty of guts. . . . I think it's got charm, and you can be intelligent and still like it."

If *Johnny Come Lately* was different from *Yankee Doodle Dandy,* so was the atmosphere on the set deliberately made different from anything at Warner Bros. For one thing, there was time for the occasional practical joke. One scene in the film was set in a small-town square. It looked like any one of the squares of a hundred American towns, complete with its own Civil War hero's statue. But Bill said the statue did not look old enough, and lacked the one thing that would make it appear genuine. So he brought in a flock of pigeons and told Jimmy he hoped they would get on with it.

Jimmy enjoyed the joke. So did his brothers Ed and Harry, who now spent most of their time apparently taking the blood pressure and temperature of everyone on the set. Harry had just moved to the West and wanted to make himself useful. Later, he and Ed would also be giving physicals to air cadets. But for the moment they were enjoying "working" in Hollywood.

Meanwhile, their youngest brother and now "boss" of the operation was assessing the qualities of the star in the family: "Jimmy," Bill said, "has a kind of electricity that makes audiences expect action from him; even the way he moves is a sort of promise. And we can't let the audience be disappointed too much. Most of Jimmy's pictures will probably be romantic pictures of some sort."

Certainly, he promised, there would be no William Cagney Productions gangster films starring Jimmy. "There'll be no more cocky arrogance of the old Warner's formula. On the positive side," he went on, "there are just a couple of simple rules:

"First, I think the duty of every producer who reads a script is to sit down and ask himself what right he has to ask a possible 20 million people to listen to the story he wants to tell. Second, don't offend your audience by assuming it's twelve years old. Therefore, you can't kid it along.

"There's another thing, too," he added. "The audience is your customer and the customer is always right, dammit. You're making pictures for them, not for yourself. Now, I've been watching Jimmy for ten years. It's kind of peculiar putting our own brother under the microscope, but that's what I've had to do—analyze what he had to sell, what he had to be careful of."

One of the things Jimmy ought to have been more careful of, the critics seemed to agree, was making films like *Johnny Come Lately*.

The New York *Post* was kind. "It is not dreadful," said their review of the film. "Cagney is still the unique Cagney—but it is far below his standard. To put it bluntly, it is an old-fashioned story told in an old-fashioned manner." The sting was in the tail of the piece: "Please, Mr. Cagney, for the benefit of the public, yourself and Warner's—go back where you made pictures like *Yankee Doodle Dandy.*"

Jimmy, however, said he had no intention of going back to Warner Bros. And, as if to prove it, he made sure that the publicity department of his new studio had his birth date right. He was forty-four now and not thirty-nine, as the Warner Bros. studio biography would have it. He didn't give a damn that he was born in 1899 and not 1904.

He was much more concerned with trying to help fight the war. *The New York Times* came out with a list of stars who were not in the forces because the law at the time exempted fathers of two or more children. Don Ameche, Bing Crosby, Joel McCrea, John Garfield, Gary Cooper, Dennis Morgan, John Wayne, and James Cagney were in the same category. As far as Jimmy was concerned, he wanted to get straight out and make his contribution to the war effort. There were, however, more useful ways of doing this than merely posing for photographs in crisp new uniforms. He was promised opportunities to go to the troops and to sell war bonds.

While he waited, he spent his time working on the farm, cleaning out the cesspools and showering down the cow stalls. "It isn't exactly fun," Jimmy conceded at the time. "But most farming is. And you just can't get hired hands these days." He was also seriously thinking about the future. "When I'm through with pictures," he forecast, "this is where I'll be—back on the farm with the cows and the chickens. There'll be no comeback in the theater for me. I wouldn't consider it for a minute." Jimmy was always determined that, once having made a promise, he was going to keep it.

Another promise he made was to be sure to keep his children out of the limelight. Many parents of adopted children worry in case a blood relative would show up and attempt to claim their youngsters or a sum of money that would send them away. The Cagneys wished to avoid such an occurrence if possible.

Jimmy and Bill used to like to spend the early war evenings talking to their friends and neighbors. One member of their intimate set called Mrs. Cagney the "Dorothy Parker of Coldwater Canyon." While Bill talked, Jimmy strummed his guitar or curled up with one of the books in his ever-growing library.

He left the selling of Cagney pictures to his brother, the company president. They both arrived in New York on the same day in 1943—brother Bill to sell *Johnny Come Lately*, Jimmy to sell war bonds. At a special bond rally, he did a *Yankee Doodle Dandy* dance routine and sang "Yip" Harburg's new song "That's What We Buy When We Buy War Bonds." He approved of the sentiment completely. He liked the work so much that even when his luggage was lost, he did not complain.

"There's one thing about the American people," he said in his best patriotic form. "We can always laugh. That's what they've found out about the boys from overseas. No matter how tough the going is, they still find something to laugh at. That's why we feel entertainment is so valuable in wartime. We've asked people from all over the country—from models to factory workers—what they want, and they all say they want to be amused."

Jimmy did his best to oblige. He tramped all over the country, selling bonds. When he was not actually selling them, he was helping other people to do so. He became chairman of Hollywood's Victory Committee, which organized camp shows and assigned the other stars to where it was considered they were needed most. The pull of a Hollywood actor in wartime was tremendous. It showed itself both directly in selling and indirectly in helping to build up morale. Four British factory employees were selected in 1943 to tour American war plants as "ambassadors" for their fellow workers. As soon as one of them, Mr. Patrick Carey, of London, arrived in the States he said he had one big ambition: "To meet James Cagney in the flesh." Jimmy was happy to play host. He showed the man around his Coldwater Canyon "victory garden," which he proudly revealed was the largest in Hollywood.

He also helped the war by lending his "pride and joy," the *Martha,* to the Coast Guard. Soon afterward, he was given the news he had been waiting for: he could go on a large-scale bond-selling and troop-entertaining tour. First he would be leading the Hollywood Victory Caravan; later he would go overseas. When the Caravan started its countrywide tour, he was accompanied by O'Brien, Merle Oberon, and a host of others. It was the toughest job he had taken on in years, but it was his kind of war service and he knew he really was doing more good than just stepping into uniform for the benefit of a crowd of photographers.

Cagney was back "on the boards" again. It was the first extended run he had had since getting on that train for California fourteen years before. He was also working harder than he had worked at any time since he and Bill were on the two-and-more-a-day vaudeville circuit.

The Caravan was, in fact, a special train in which the artists sang and danced to each other in the middle of the cars, told each other stories as the evenings drew into nights. Inevitably, they sometimes also quarreled. But the humor was mostly good.

In terms of discomfort, the train *was* like a desert caravan. For three days, there were no clean towels on board, and Cagney, Pat O'Brien, and Frank McHugh shared the use of one of Jimmy's old sweat shirts.

En route, Jimmy sang "You're a Grand Old Flag" and

"Yankee Doodle Boy" standing on makeshift platforms in old tumbledown halls. Frequently, to reach his dressing room he had to walk on duck boards thrown across barrels in the mud. That dressing room was usually a convenient place for everyone else in the cast, too—big star or chorus girl—to get together after a show. In one place, they all *had* to use his room. It was the only way they had to get to their own rooms from the stage. To keep everyone happy, a girl distributed free sandwiches and orangeade—making it all rather resemble the famous stateroom scene from the Marx Brothers film *A Night at the Opera*. "We never did find out who that girl was," Jimmy joked.

Neither did the Caravaners ever come to terms with the sort of hotel accommodation they were offered. Their rooms were small, stuffy, and noisy. When Pat O'Brien saw the room he had been allocated in Washington, D.C., one member of the troupe reported: "You could hear him holler in New Rochelle." And Bert Lahr, frequently an honorary member of the "Irish Mafia," said he felt he went to bed every night he was on the Caravan feeling he was in an iron lung.

But there was no doubt that the money raised by the Caravan justified the inconveniences. Each performance was reckoned to have brought in between $50,000 and $82,000. A man named Epstein traveled with the performers with the brief that he look after the receipts. When the shows finally came to their end, no one was looking more miserable than Mr. Epstein.

"What's wrong, Eppy?" Cagney asked him.

"I've got to go back to the Plymouth Theater after this is all over," he answered. "And if anyone slips me $91 after a Saturday night's business, I'm going to bust him over the head."

The camaraderie of the Caravaners was something special, if not unique. All taking part realized they were helping the war and they all seemed to want to do that. When it was all over, Jimmy went to the Vineyard to try to recuperate. "We just looked at each other and we knew that there never was a troupe like that and never would be again," he said, thinking about the work they had all been putting in.

He was soon going off to England to entertain the troops readying for D-Day. But before he went, there was time to relax, helping Bill in the house, working out with his animals on the farm, and occasionally watching horses at the track. In Long Island he was called upon to present the Hambleton Trophy to W. H. Strang, owner of the horse Ambassador. Three days later, he donned a set of racing silks himself and drove in an exhibition race of trotting horses. His horse Watching finished second to Mrs. Neville Applegate's Hanover Express. Having acquitted himself more than respectably, he got down to the serious business of the day, taking over the microphone and selling more bonds.

For the moment, William Cagney Productions Inc., were keeping their top star on ice—giving him time to make a March of Time documentary for Twentieth Century-Fox called *Show Business at War.* Bette Davis, Humphrey Bogart, Ginger Rogers, Jack Benny, Bob Hope, and Gertrude Lawrence were with him, too, all showing how they were helping to fight the war on screen. In 1943 he also starred as an air-raid warden in a short called *You, John Jones.* In eight minutes, Cagney, his screen wife Ann Sothern, and Margaret O'Brien as their daughter showed their idea of life in a Japanese-occupied America.

Hollywood was making him their typical "Mr. Good Film Star." In November 1943, as if to prove it, he was reelected president of the Screen Actors Guild. In January 1944 he sailed for Britain with Fred Astaire, Bing Crosby, and Mickey Rooney. The USO, which organized the tour, described the group as "the biggest bunch of Hollywood stars ever to come here."

They were traveling under strict Army orders and in Army uniforms. On the troopship—he had promised Bill he would not break their pact and fly without her—they suffered the privations of the other troops. They had cramped quarters, they fought for room on the crowded decks. But they tried to make the journey go as smoothly as possible without seeming to rush the men to the prospective battle line. Jimmy himself organized twelve shows for the troops on board. "And it was darned good theater," he said afterward.

There were certain privileges for the stars. Jimmy had been booked into London's plush Mayfair Hotel and was promised time off to attend the premiere of *Johnny Vagabond,* as *Johnny Come Lately* was being called in Britain.

But first he had to get to Britain. The ship was late docking at Southampton—so late that the USO publicity department had to issue a statement saying: "They have started their journey across the Atlantic. Nothing has happened as far as we know. Delays do sometimes occur, you know." After Jimmy finally did arrive at a port "somewhere in England," there were further delays on the trip to London. His car ran out of gas, and Jimmy and his entourage missed the midnight dinner planned for them at the hotel.

When the tour started, Jimmy had a new routine perfected for the men "over there." He did an Irish clog dance—to emphasize, he pointed out, that he could entertain without a gun—and in those days he was certain his audiences had seen enough of guns and at altogether too close quarters. He also gave priority to entertaining in military hospitals—"because I believe entertainment has a definite therapeutic value for sick people."

The London *Evening Standard* reported that when he began talking to the troops, he was "in a mild, serious mood." But he took every opportunity for a gag just the same. "There was a guy who came up to me," he told the troops. "He said there was no room for both of us around the place. One of us had to go. I went."

He planned to do twelve shows a week, plus his hospital visits. In the end, that output was almost doubled. He loved every minute of this brand of entertaining.

To perfect his clog dancing, he took instruction from Johnny O'Biyle, an American dancer who had lectured on the evolution of dancing at American universities. He was going to develop his act to show how modern tap dancing had really come not only from Irish jigs but from the Lancashire clog dances, too.

He also planned to go to Ireland to see where his ancestors had hailed from. The only thing worrying him was that he didn't think he had any relatives still living there.

Not everyone was happy that James Cagney really was working solely for the war effort. Some papers suggested that he and the other entertainers on the tour were seeking personal publicity. The charge angered Jimmy. "Actors and actresses," he declared, "have just one purpose. And that is to do the job."

As part of that job he went on the stage of London's Palace Theatre and led 1400 voices of boys of the British Army Cadet Force singing "Yankee Doodle Boy." The boys had been chosen because of their good conduct.

Naturally enough, he could not completely avoid being spotted by the cameras. The Army Signal Corps made a short motion picture of rehearsals for the tour and it went around Army camps all over the world.

For the British people, it was their first opportunity to watch him in the flesh. One woman reporter was struck that he has "blue eyes beneath his straight, beetling brows and freckles. He has got a friendly smile, but he is rather reserved."

Entertaining at the various bases, Cagney's vaudeville background was paying a heap of dividends. On one occasion in March 1944, he was playing at a bomber station in Northern England during an air raid. Just as the second act of his show got going, the sound of gunfire could be heard coming from fairly close at hand. "I'm no expert at this sort of thing," said Jimmy as he walked onto the stage. "But I think the general idea is to get out of here." Everyone did—and roared with laughter while doing so. They left the makeshift theater just as it was struck by what sounded like a loud explosion. It turned out to be the fuel tank of a crashing Junkers 88.

Jimmy quipped: "Back in the States, I had a fight to get two gallons of the stuff a week. Over here, Hitler sends us a tankful—by special delivery." The audience was his for the rest of the hour he was on stage.

He was beginning to love his tour of Britain and Ireland. Predictably, it was the countryside that enchanted him the most. He stopped his car to talk to farmers about the problems of wartime crop-growing and sent for a notebook in which he would record some tips he was taking back to the Vineyard with him. His most rewarding visit was with a group of thatchers, and he extracted from them a promise to let him thatch a cottage. Later on, he had plans to learn how to make a "nice tidy hayrick."

But then in April 1944, all the fun was gone. His mother was suddenly taken seriously ill and he had to rush back to the States.

Carrie, the perfect mother, lay paralyzed on her bed when Jimmy reached her side. Soon afterward, she died. The Cagney matriarch and the biggest single influence in the lives of all her children had left behind her a tremendous void.

When life began to settle down again, William Cagney

Productions announced its shooting schedule for the near future. They were going into a program of six pictures in conjunction with United Artists—with Jimmy starring in five of them. The company vice-president announced, however, that that did not rule out his working for any other studio—but the proposition would have to be extremely tempting for him to do so. Dozens of offers came in, but because none of them measured up to his own idea of perfection, they were all rejected.

The company felt they were right to so insist. Already *Johnny Come Lately* had grossed $2.3 million, which was easily $1 million of clear profit. Warner Bros., meanwhile, happily revealed that *Yankee Doodle Dandy* had notched up profits in the $6 million range.

The first of Jimmy's new films, he and his brother decided, was to be called *Blood on the Sun,* a propaganda exercise against the Japanese at what was considered to be the perfect time. In this, Jimmy once more played a newspaperman, but this time in the Tokyo of the late 1920's. He discovers that the mysterious deaths of a group of Japanese friends are connected with their government's plans to become the master race of the East.

Cast opposite him was Sylvia Sidney, and that casting gave cause to the first row since Jimmy had joined the new organization. The script called for him to slap Miss Sidney's face, but he refused to do it. "That stuff's out," he declared —and this time he had power to make sure it really was out. In doing so, however, he found himself at odds with his publicity department—always the *bête noir,* as far as he was concerned, in a studio. They had put out a statement by Miss Sidney saying she really did not at all care about being hit. "What's good enough for his other women is good enough for me," they proudly quoted her as saying.

The London *Times,* not the easiest newspaper to please,

liked *Blood on the Sun*. The paper's anonymous critic quoted a line from the film: " 'You are so intensely alive,' says Miss Sylvia Sidney to Mr. James Cagney during the fast-moving film of Tokyo in the days of 1928 and it is impossible not to agree with her."

Variety agreed completely: "The stars of this picture are given plenty of opportunity to display their histrionics. Cagney is the same rough-and-tumble character he's always been."

For some in Hollywood, Jimmy had become a bit too rough-and-tumble, and not just in his films. The right-wingers still did not like his politics. When he came out for President Roosevelt against Governor Dewey in the 1944 election, a sizable number of film-colony personalities were lined up against him—particularly the Hollywood-for-Dewey Committee, sponsored jointly by Lionel Barrymore, Ginger Rogers, and Bing Crosby.

Nobody ever came to blows, but there were the occasional embarrassing moments, none more so than the dinner organized by the Free World Association, which Cagney had supported amid comments that it was "leftist." Among its other members were Rosalind Russell, Charles Boyer, and Rochester, Jack Benny's gentleman's gentleman. One night they were holding a dinner in honor of then vice-president Henry Wallace—it was early in the campaign and he had not yet been dropped from the Roosevelt ticket—at the plush Beverly Wilshire Hotel in Beverly Hills.

The same evening, a right-wing group led by Walt Disney and Gary Cooper held another dinner at the Beverly Hills Hotel. Unfortunately for good political organization, the motorcycle cop escorting the vice-president had the hotels confused—and before anyone could realize what had happened the right-wingers had Henry Wallace as their guest by default.

But Jimmy took his allegiance to Roosevelt very seriously.

With Humphrey Bogart, Deanna Durbin, Katharine Hepburn, Bette Davis, Olivia de Havilland, and his "Yankee Doodle father" Walter Huston, he signed a declaration of support: "Roosevelt," they all declared, "is vital to the security of our country and its place in the postwar world."

When that postwar period began, Jimmy was determined to size up to any new conditions with which he would be faced. But he was also going to try to get more time for himself—and for Bill and the kids.

16 CEILING ZERO

THE CHANGES in the film industry were latent in 1945. Newcomers had arrived from war service and were talking about the plans they had for a more serious and responsible Hollywood. But Warner Bros. and the other moguls simply wanted a speedy return to the profitable past and, at first, took little notice. Their big aim was to keep the running of the "asylum" out of the hands of the "inmates."

Jimmy, the inmate who had escaped, would like to have fled from the film scene altogether, but he kept on working to make *13 Rue Madeleine*. Unfortunately, it was greeted with a certain amount of skepticism. One critic wrote: "I refuse to be as respectful as the film demands at the sight of James Cagney keeping the secret of D-Day from the Germans practically single-handed." For the first time, people were thinking about Cagney and reacting to him in the way they had for years been smirking about Errol Flynn. It was particularly galling because Jimmy worked harder than almost any other Hollywood actor just to make his portrayals believable. In *13 Rue Madeleine*, we had to imagine he was sitting in a chair under Gestapo interrogation when he knew that at any moment, Allied bombers were going to blow both him and his captors sky-high. Nothing would make the captive divulge his big secret. You did not have to accept the full concept as laid down in the film, but you could not fail to respect the mastery of Cagney's performance.

Whether it was because of the way *13 Rue Madeleine* was received or simply because he was exhausted from the buildup of all the pressures of recent years, he decided in 1946 to call a temporary stop. He went back to the farm and sailed his yacht. On the farm, he found out more about handling tractors and about the horses that were very much a part of his life. On his yacht, he was an experienced as well as a keen sailor. But he was not so proficient on one occasion. He was out on the *Martha* when the winds dropped so low that the boat was completely becalmed. The Coast Guard had to help him back to port.

Film offers continued to come into the offices of William Cagney Productions, but they were studied by Bill Cagney and turned down. By the end of 1946, Jimmy's earnings were down by a third from the 1941 figure, but he did not worry about it and went back to the things he considered important. Then, in 1948, he went back to the family firm.

The Time of Your Life seemed to meet most of the requirements the Cagney brothers had laid down. It had a fascinating story idea with plenty of opportunities for Jimmy to shine as a "character." It was also a story Jimmy knew well. It had been written by William Saroyan and had had a successful Broadway run. Cagney had seen it and he felt that slight tug of envy which made him, momentarily, wish he were still a stage actor. Now he did have the opportunity to interpret the role of a kind of emcee in the way he felt he could do best.

The film was about a group of people in a San Francisco

waterfront bar talking about the dreams they know will never be fulfilled. To these perpetual Walter Mittys, Jimmy is counselor and listener. He listened with equal tact and understanding to the peroxide blonde (his sister Jeanne in one of her best performances), to James Barton, who said he was Kit Carson the Wild West folk hero, Broderick Crawford as a policeman, and William Bendix playing the part of the barman that he created in the Broadway version. All the time the habitués are spinning their yarns, and the focus switches from one to the other, Jimmy is with them.

It was a difficult film to make. The problems were similar to the ones Eugene O'Neill faced with his *The Iceman Cometh:* how to ensure that the right people had the necessary attention at the right time. Saroyan solved the problem in the original play by giving them sufficiently strong dialogue. That alone would not turn it into a successful film. The Cagneys rightly agreed that there was but one way to hope that could happen and that was by their selection of director. They chose one of the most skilled men in Hollywood, H. C. "Hank" Potter.

What struck Potter, working on the film, was the ease with which Jimmy took direction and never—almost alone among big stars in this—tried to force his own ideas on the director. As number two man in the studio, he could have insisted upon his status and turned Potter into a mere cipher.

Potter was allowed to get on with his job and in turn paid Jimmy the compliment of being a good actor, giving him situations he could master to the best advantage. "He was never a ham," Potter recalls today.

To get around the difficulties in the screenplay, Potter spent hours making sure the camera angles were in every way the most suitable. In return, Cagney made sure that he was always word-perfect, that his speeches were ready and learned by the time he turned up on the set early in the morning.

The only difficulties of any note were from the producer. William Cagney was more and more turning into a backroom boy in the outfit, leaving much of the production work to his director. When he did get involved and didn't like what he saw happening, he flew into what the people in the studio began to call his "wild Irish temper."

When *The Time of Your Life* was completed, no one was happier with the results than the author. William Saroyan took the almost unheard-of step of sending Potter a telegram, congratulating him on what he had managed to do with his "almost unmanageable material."

The press was less enthusiastic about *The Time of Your Life* than Hank Potter and the Cagneys. The New York *World Telegram* called it "a collection of great moments set in a string of lulls.... Cagney and his director H. C. Potter simply assembled a set of good actors and let them cut loose on their odd Saroyan characters."

Jimmy, of course, never allowed himself to "cut loose." His work was far too important. He did it either well or not at all. But he was always able to leave the studio behind at the end of a day. H. C. Potter had dinner with him on a number of occasions during the making of *The Time of Your Life* and was impressed by how little stock he put in being the life and soul of the party. "You'd never imagine he was an actor," he told me.

When the film was finally in the can and he could take off for the Vineyard, Jimmy sat back and did what he playfully said he liked doing best of all—"spending a week debating whether or not I set a new fencepost, decide against it, and then go fishing."

When he got back to work and joined his brother in the William Cagney Productions board room, there was serious talking to do. The brothers made what was perhaps their hardest decision of all since Jimmy had completed *Yankee Doodle Dandy:* he was going back to Warner Bros.—only this time willingly.

It was a moment of supreme irony. The Cagneys had actually talked to Jack L. Warner and decided they wanted to come back. But the terms they agreed to now were different from any others they had made. This time, it was going to be a partnership.

The trouble had been that the Cagneys were finding it increasingly difficult getting United Artists to provide the necessary money to distribute Jimmy's films. When the brothers tried to work out who could find the cash, they were drawn to the inescapable conclusion that only Warner Bros. had the required resources.

The new contract between Warner's and the Cagney organization specified that they could get out whenever they wanted to—and that all the takings would be split down the middle. No specific picture deals were yet contemplated, but it was agreed that they would be shot at the General Service Studios, which the Cagneys leased.

Most important of all, Bill Cagney revealed, Jack Warner was promising "full autonomy" to Jimmy and himself. In other words, they were now declaring official the situation that had been forced upon them when they were making *Yankee Doodle Dandy.*

The deal was concluded in late 1947. But it was not until 1949 that the first film was made under the new arrangement. Its title: *White Heat.*

17 WHITE HEAT

AROUND Hollywood, they spoke of *White Heat* as a comeback. Not just a comeback to Warner Bros., but to the sort of part in which he had had his biggest successes. It was Cagney in his old gangster mold, punching, shoving, shooting his way through the picture and dropping more than a few goodies as he did so.

The film was also predicted to be the start of a whole new gangster era, with all the sophistication that improved direction and photography techniques could bring to it. But if the gangster film did not come back, the old Cagney did. And he discovered a whole new generation of filmgoers who liked seeing him in his old screen environment.

As he had always done in the past, he took the dialogue given to him by his writers—this time Ivan Goff and Ben Roberts—and honed it to suit the character he saw himself playing. In this case, he was playing a hijacker called Cody Jarrett whose biggest difficulty in life was not so much his predilection for crime as his abnormal love for his mother.

Cagney improvised his dialogue, added touches to a

number of the scenes, and decided that the Cody Jarrett he would play would make a lot more sense if he also suffered blinding migraines. He knew that the onset of one of those headaches would provide an opportunity to seethe and writhe as he had not been able to do since the days of *The Public Enemy*.

What his director Raoul Walsh knew equally well was that Cagney could be relied upon to dramatize each jab of pain to the point that people in the audience would be close to searching for their own aspirin bottles. Cagney did that and more, but always without reaching the stage where it looked as if he were overacting. As he threw epileptic fits, moaned, and squirmed, he was really reliving one of the unhappiest moments of his life—when his friend took him for a treat to the insane asylum at Ward's Island.

There were moments in the film when it is difficult to imagine anyone else carrying off what he was now able to do. The times when he is with his mother (Margaret Wycherly in a superb performance) are among them. At one stage, he even sits on her lap. Almost any other actor would have made it look laughable. Cagney makes it seem never less than a poignant gesture of filial devotion. But Jimmy admits he had his doubts about being able to do it successfully. It was not in the script, but he put the idea to Walsh. "Just let's see if we can get away with it," he told him. They tried, and get away with it he did.

The scene was not his only contribution to the story line. Once more, he kicks his leading lady—this time Virginia Mayo, trying to live down her role as the sex symbol in the many Danny Kaye comedies. Jimmy decided that there was only one way to win the battle of the sexes and that was by implied sex. Once having struck her, he grabs Virginia, puts her over his shoulder, and carts her up the stairs to bed. Even with a trim leading lady like her, that took strength.

One of the interesting features of the film was that a new generation was involved on the set as well as in the audience. One of them was Edmond O'Brien, and he was able to painlessly appreciate the Cagney strength. Once Jimmy lunged against him, it would have taken the power of an all-in wrestler to release his grip. But he did not hurt O'Brien.

It was the gentle Cagney, in fact, who made the biggest impression on O'Brien. When the lights were up and the camera was turning, Cagney looked like an angry tiger. But as soon as shooting came to a temporary stop, he could say in a pleading whisper: "Say, would you mind telling me what you think of this?" "This" turned out to be a short but quite beautiful poem which Jimmy had written while waiting to be called to the floor. When the actors went back to work, he would make another plea: "Please, don't tell anyone about it."

The generous side of Cagney was also seen in the studio. O'Brien played an FBI man placed, in order to try to recover some vital information, in the prison where Cody is held. They were playing a close-up scene together when suddenly O'Brien noticed a pressure on top of his right foot. All the time that Cagney was going through his speech and getting ready to use his fists, the pressure increased. It was not called for in the script. It had not been discussed in any studio conference, but Jimmy was pressing harder than ever, without moving a muscle in his face. And then O'Brien realized why. If he had not moved around, as Cagney was in this way telling him to do, he would have been out of frame and Jimmy would have had the scene to himself. Dozens of other actors would have grabbed that opportunity to steal the scene. Cagney knew it belonged as much to O'Brien as to himself and saw no reason to claim what was not rightfully his.

The most moving moment in the film is when O'Brien and Cagney are sitting with all the other convicts at the prison meal table. Suddenly, there is a hush all around them. The word goes from one to the other until it finally reaches Jimmy: "Your Ma is dead." At first, Cagney simply looks down. Years later, he explained to Charles Champlin in the Los Angeles *Times:* "That first agony is private. If I'd looked up right away and started bellowing, it would have been stock company, 1912."

But he did not look down for long. Soon he was in a mad frenzy (which would also one day be food for his imitators). He did not merely cry. It was as if heated needles were being slowly pushed under his fingernails. He went berserk, running wildly around the massive hall.

Before the film ends, Cody Jarrett has escaped and is involved in a serious robbery. The police catch up with him and track him down to an oil refinery. He stands on top of the tower as guns are focused on him from below, bullets flying everywhere. One reaches its target. But before he dies, he gets ready to shoot a bullet into the tank and finally blow himself and everything around him sky-high. As he prepares to die, he shouts: "Made it, Ma. Top of the world!"

The film was to have an amazing impact on audiences. But the response was sometimes too enthusiastic in Jimmy's view. On one of the rare occasions that Jimmy went to a theater to see one of his own films, he was approached by a small boy in the crowd, who asked if he could shake his idol's hand. Jimmy was happy to oblige.

"Gee, I sure enjoyed your picture," he told him.

Instead of being pleased by the child's admiration, Jimmy confessed he was shocked. "What does your mother think of your seeing a picture like this?" he asked.

The boy answered: "Oh, she liked it as much as I did."

Jimmy was last seen disappearing into the crowd and muttering: "Well, don't blame me."

He had a strong social conscience about the effect of his

work on the younger members of the population. He wondered whether it was right to keep making that sort of movie. But he thought: "Hoodlums remain the same dumb braggarts while crime prevention and detective methods advance along with science. It's a great thing for some of the elements in the youth of a nation to realize."

In *The New York Times,* Bosley Crowther gave one of the most perceptive assessments of his career when he said of Jimmy's performance in *White Heat:* "Mr. Cagney plays it with such dynamic arrogance, such beautiful laying out of detail, that he gives the whole picture a high charge."

That also seems to be the impression that Winston Churchill had of *White Heat.* When Raoul Walsh flew into London in October 1949, he had with him a print of the picture. He took it straight to Chartwell, the home of the great wartime prime minister, who was now leader of the Opposition. That evening they saw *White Heat* together and Churchill was reported to have loved every gripping moment. He always said that Cagney and the Marx Brothers were his favorite performers.

Paul Holt in the London *Daily Herald* was as pleased with the picture as were most other people. He wrote: "Fred Astaire dancing. Wallace Beery squinting one eye. Garbo's sniff. Clark Gable's silly smile and Cagney's lightning fist are the things you remember in a decade's film going—and Cagney's fist (bless it) is here with us again after years of rest."

The *Times* of London was more restrained: "Mr. Cagney is never less than an actor of experience and competence who knows precisely what he is doing. The trouble is that this particular part is one he knows all too well."

When filming of *White Heat* was completed, the first thing Cagney did was go out on his boat with his wife Bill and their children. Before they left the Coldwater Canyon house, however, Jimmy got on the phone and called Edmond O'Brien.

"Get the Spaniard," he instructed, referring to O'Brien's new wife, dancer Olga St. Juan, "and we'll all go out on the yacht."

Jimmy was always proud of his boat. When the guests drove up to its moorings, he showed them the vessel with pride. Around them were a dozen or more fans who shouted words of greeting. When they got aboard, everything looked set for a good trip. People in nearby boats shouted "Bon voyage" and Jimmy was in seventh heaven. And then it happened. The mast snapped, and sails came tumbling down on to the deck. As O'Brien now recalls with a well-meaning chuckle: "Poor old Jimmy wanted to die there and then in front of ten million people!"

He made it up to the disappointed O'Brien a few days later, however. He rang him again from the Coldwater Canyon house, and issued an invitation: "Say, Irish. How about you coming over and we have just one?"

O'Brien got into his car and joined Jimmy for just that "one"—a single glass of whatever he fancied that night. To the younger actor that was a signal tribute from a near-abstainer, an indication that Jimmy had enjoyed working with him.

Cagney was always loyal to the people with whom he was associated. He now had two new farms, one near Los Angeles in the Valley, the other in Dutchess County, New York. Staying with the Cagney family in New York in March 1950 was Jack Sergel, a former police wrestling champion who was sometimes referred to as Jimmy's bodyguard. It seemed a convenient arrangement the night that an intruder broke into the house. Sergel rounded on him and discovered he was Kenneth Kuniyuki, the Cagneys' former butler and himself a Japanese-style wrestling expert. Kuniyuki, it appeared, had forced his way into the house in an attempt to see his estranged wife Elizabeth. Cagney, as loyal as ever, had encouraged Elizabeth to stay on in the house even though her butler husband had left. Whether

Jimmy needed Mr. Sergel's help or not is a matter for conjecture. But while Kuniyuki was with him, Jimmy learned judo and gained a first-degree belt.

Two months after that encounter, Jimmy dealt personally with another intruder—this time in California. He heard a noise coming from the hills and thought it ominous. The countryman in him recognized the call of a coyote on the prowl and he was anxious that a potential killer of that kind should not be allowed to hurt nearby livestock. Jimmy jumped out of bed, hoping Bill would not hear, and grabbed the gun he kept by him for security. He ran off in his pajamas toward where he believed the animal was now in hiding. But he stumbled, the gun went off and grazed his hand. "It's just a scratch," he later told reporters. But he promised to be more careful in the future.

18 WHAT PRICE GLORY?

THE second half of the twentieth century opened with Jimmy preparing to hoof once more. And he looked happier at the prospect than he had about any other film for years. He was thrilled by the reactions he had had to *White Heat* and was now looking forward to doing what he really enjoyed doing best—making a musical.

Because he had veto powers over all the projects submitted to him, Jimmy really has only himself to blame for *The West Point Story*. He grabbed it because it was a musical with an amusing story, and he was feeling healthy enough to dance with as much enthusiasm and energy as he had done in *Yankee Doodle Dandy*. If nothing else, dancing gave him a splendidly disciplined way of keeping his weight down.

But *The West Point Story* did little else for him. It was the story of a Broadway musical director, now on hard times, who agrees to put on the annual "100th Night" show at West Point Academy—and ends up dressing like a cadet. It would be hard to imagine anyone less like a West Point cadet in 1950 than the fifty-one-year-old James Cagney. As far as can be discovered, in his day nobody from Yorkville had a West Point education. So he did what only Cagney and perhaps a select few other actors would have done: he went down to the academy with producer Louis F. Edelman, ate with the cadets, and slept there, too.

Jimmy was intensely enthusiastic in the dance numbers, wearing—when he was not in uniform—a now very dated wide-shouldered suit, narrow bow tie, and huge brimmed hat. He worked so hard in the final chorus, making so many knee skids as he danced with arms outstretched toward the cameras, that his legs felt like damp pulp.

Virginia Mayo was once more cast as his girl friend, and there was an early Doris Day looking pretty. Among the other period talent in the film were Gordon MacRae and Gene Nelson. But *The West Point Story* looked too much like *The Chocolate Soldier*—without the chocolate.

Bosley Crowther in *The New York Times* wrote: "If everything about *The West Point Story* were anywhere near as good as Jimmy Cagney is in it, this Warner musical show would be the top musical of the year. For the estimable Mr. Cagney is in rare good form in this film, singing, dancing and wisecracking in his most electrifying style and putting on a show of braggadocio that makes one tingle with gleeful delight." The trouble was, Mr. Crowther reported, the rest of the picture was nowhere near as good as the "estimable Mr. Cagney."

Jimmy was so disappointed with the picture that he now seriously considered retiring for good. When his friend Robert Montgomery asked him to join his television show, he politely asked for a rain check.

His next picture, released as a William Cagney Production for Warner Bros.–First National, was hardly more successful. *Kiss Tomorrow Goodbye* had Jimmy back to his old tricks, slapping the curvy Barbara Payton around with a rolled-up wet towel. Luther Adler and Ward Bond were in the film, and Bill Cagney even gave himself a small role—as Jimmy's brother. But it added up to the studio's throwing everything it had into a poor picture.

There was so much violence in the picture—shooting and punching as well as the fight with Miss Payton—that there was trouble again with the censors in Ohio. The film was banned from the state because it was considered to be a "sordid, sadistic presentation of brutality."

But Jimmy decided not to let it get him down. He took his Bill and the kids back to one of the farms and worried about painting more fences. He had another two Warner Bros. films planned, but not until 1951.

Warner Bros. continued to put out press releases about their big star, who they said was now forty-six years old. Despite his own frequent denials, the old studio still insisted that he was born in 1904. He tried not to let it bother him any more than did the publication of the top crowd pullers for 1950. This showed that Jimmy was no longer among them.

Early in 1951 he tried to update *The Lost Weekend* story with a new film about an alcoholic journalist trying to reform a younger drinking reporter. *Come Fill the Cup* was as unhappy a choice of film as the others of the new decade. It featured Gig Young, Raymond Massey, and James Gleason, but somehow it just confirmed the view that Jimmy did a much better job acting in films than he did in choosing his material.

Come Fill the Cup was full of cinematic clichés. Cagney's performance as a one-man Alcoholics Anonymous was as brilliant as usual, but people were by now beginning to get tired of brilliant tours de force submerged by a morass of hokum.

The year's second Cagney-Warner film, *Starlift,* was the most disastrous of all. He was lost in a crowd of other Hollywood stars supposedly entertaining men at an airbase awaiting transport to Korea. Doris Day, Gary Cooper, Jane Wyman, Ruth Roman, and Gordon MacRae all suffered because they were available for the film. It insulted every one of them.

There was only one Cagney film in 1952. By the time it was released, some people wondered whether there was anything symbolic about the title, *What Price Glory?* Jimmy, who still preferred the farm, could have done better than risk the suggestions it conjured up. John Ford directed the picture and it was probably one of his worst, too. The price of remaking the old World War I story—with Dan Dailey and Corinne Calvet co-starring with Cagney—was all too high. The New York *Morning Telegraph* even noted that Jimmy had a paunch.

He spent more time than ever now on the farms with the family. When his brother Bill was married, everyone in the Cagney clan rejoiced. When their sister Jeanne was divorced a fortnight later from actor Kim Spaulding (also known as Ross F. Latimer) she, too, had to call upon the family with Jimmy as its cornerstone.

For Jimmy himself there was still only one thing that gave him as much pleasure as being able to work or relax on the farm and that was sailing his boat. He now had a new one, the *Mary Ann.* In 1953, three complete strangers had reason to be glad that he did have it—and that he also knew how to handle it. He was sailing the ketch off the New England coast when he saw a small sailing boat come toward him and then suddenly capsize. He raced for the boat and, with great difficulty, managed to rescue its three occupants from the rough sea. When the men had dried off, Jimmy extracted a promise from each of them: that they would never reveal what had happened.

It was not until 1956 that one of the men felt he could hold his silence no longer and an embarrassed Cagney had finally to confess his part in the rescue. "I thought it sounded too contrived," he said in explanation for his reticence. "Too Hollywood."

It is possible that the United States government felt much the same way when they received Jimmy's income tax allowance claims. They refused to allow him to deduct $5414 for dancing lessons and massages in 1950. No one denied he had had all the things he claimed. They just did not think they were the sort of things that should be regarded as deductible.

When Jimmy went back to work in 1953, he at last had a film that was worthy of him. *A Lion Is in the Streets* could have been made six years earlier—when William Cagney Productions had first bought the property. "But I'm very glad that we didn't," said Jimmy; "1947 was the year the bottom fell out of the movie market."

One of the reasons the film wasn't made until 1953 was its similarity to the Huey Long story. But since Broderick Crawford had already starred in what appeared to be the Huey Long story—*All the King's Men*—it was obviously politic to deny that the Cagney screenplay was even remotely connected with a real-life unscrupulous politician. Bill produced the picture and even his brother Ed was on the staff, as story editor. To complete the family pattern of the enterprise Jeanne was in it, too, in a cameo role.

If the state of the movie market was the main reason for not making the film in 1947, things in 1953 were not that much better. The effects of television were really beginning to be felt for the first time and the industry was searching for any means it could find to regain its old position in entertainment from 3-D wide screen. Cagney's formula was his usual one, an outstanding performance. But the crowds kept away just the same.

The picture was, however, one of the best from the Cagney stable in years. Bosley Crowther called it "a headlong and dramatic drama."

The next Cagney drama was his first Western since *The Oklahoma Kid* in 1939. *Run for Cover* in 1955 was better than most Westerns about at the time, but Bosley Crowther raised a point that had never been considered in a Cagney picture before. He said that Jimmy was "cocky and colorful" but he also regretted there was not enough "substance or strenuous sincerity."

Lack of sincerity was something that had never previously been alleged about Cagney. In case anyone thought that was true, Jimmy was going to spend the next year or so working harder on the screen than he had done for years.

19 SOMETHING TO SING ABOUT

CAGNEY was about to play the most unredeemedly unpleasant character in his whole career.

Through the years, Cagney characters had pulled hair, slapped, punched, kicked, and killed—not to mention using a grapefruit in an unorthodox way. But most of them had had a sense of humor and a charm that set them apart from other people's conception of gangsters and murderers.

Marty "the Gimp" Snyder, the main character of *Love Me or Leave Me,* had no charm, no humor, no polish. There was nothing about him that made an audience want to identify with him. He was a crude brute. If anyone did sympathize with him it was because he walked with a limp. But to Jimmy, the Gimp was a character he could understand, and he turned in a fabulous performance. He played second fiddle in the picture to Doris Day—the first time he had forgone star billing since *The Millionaire*—but it was worth it. The part won him an Academy Award nomination.

The film was made by MGM. Jimmy was no longer tied

either to Warner Bros. or to William Cagney Productions, ever since the youngest of the Cagney brothers decided he could make more money that way. *Love Me or Leave Me* was the story of Ruth Etting, the "Ten Cents a Dance" girl of the Charleston era. Doris Day was both beautiful and moving in the Etting part. But, with the role of her insanely jealous husband, it was Cagney's film all the way, from the moment he entered the scene until the final credits.

It was basically a true story about a girl singing in backstreet Chicago cafes who goes right to the top on Broadway, thanks mainly to the way her crippled husband schools her. But he also attacks her, and anyone else he thinks may be getting in his way. He shoots her accompanist Johnny Alderman (played by Cameron Mitchell) when he believes the young man is paying too much attention to her.

To make sure the film was reasonably true to life, the real Gimp and the real Johnny Alderman were on hand as advisers. Jimmy consulted Snyder to help get the feel of the man—and then he consulted his own doctor brothers to find out about that limp. They told him that it appeared to them to have been caused by an injury at birth. If that were so, Jimmy decided, that alone must have made the Gimp extremely bitter. Once he understood that, he could play the part more truthfully—and he did.

William K. Zinsser in the New York *Herald Tribune* wrote: "Cagney has created a fascinating portrait of 'The Gimp.' In every mannerism—heavy limp, coarse speech, taunting sarcasm, flashes of rage—he makes an obnoxious character who tramples over everybody in his lust for power. Yet there is something pitiable about him. A look of childish bewilderment clouds his face when he finds that people don't like him or that he can't buy the love of the girl he has strong-armed to fame. It's a high tribute to Cagney that he makes this twisted man steadily interesting for two hours."

Unfortunately, one of the most interesting episodes in the Gimp's life with Ruth Etting was omitted. In the twenties, at the height of her fame, he accompanied his wife to England for a vaudeville engagement. While she was on stage, he sat in the audience with a gun trained on the orchestra leader—to make sure he did not interfere with her arrangements.

The picture was unusual in several ways. For one thing it was Jimmy's first in Cinemascope. For another, it was the first Doris Day film in which she appeared in her underwear—just a slip, but enough for the girl-next-door to feel that her image was in danger. "I have never done anything like this before," she said afterward. "Never even shown my legs in a film." She said she felt "almost ashamed" but was glad that for once she didn't have to smile all the time.

Jimmy's only comment when people asked him about the wisdom of playing yet another gangster was: "It's what the people want me to do. Someday, though, I'd like to make just one picture that the kids could go see."

He had an idea to make a picture of Thorne Smith's story "The Stray Lamb," but he thought it would be too costly. "The expense of making movies these days—wide screens, high wages—and for this picture, we would also need kids and kangaroos. Kangaroos!"

With *Love Me or Leave Me* out of the way he was most interested in going back to one of the farms. He was experimenting with raising a new strain of trotting horses, and that now excited him more than the idea of making a picture.

When he heard people talk once more of a Cagney comeback, he scratched his head and commented: "Okay. So I haven't made a picture for a while. But then, who has?" He was ignoring *Run for Cover,* which was perhaps wise. "There's been some changes round here lately, you know. Besides, there are plenty of other crazy ways to earn a living. Acting's just one way."

He and Bill left their kids behind in Beverly Hills and sailed for the South Pacific. It was not quite a second honeymoon—they had never really had a first, for that matter—for as soon as the ship docked at Midway Island, Jimmy was back at work. He was there to play another secondary role, this time in a film adaptation of the Broadway hit *Mister Roberts*.

He was playing the captain of a forgotten Navy cargo boat sailing somewhere in the Pacific—a martinet who read the comic papers and had a tree growing in a bucket on the ship's deck. He is hated by his untidy, dispirited crew, who never get shore leave. Jimmy said afterward that he based his characterization on a New England sea captain he once knew.

The title part of Lieutenant (Junior Grade) Roberts was played by Henry Fonda, who had created the role on Broadway. The ship's doctor was played, in a marvelous farewell to the screen, by William Powell. But, in all fairness, it was Jack Lemmon who made the real impact in the picture as young Ensign Pulver, who sees his twin aims in life as bringing a girl to his cabin and his captain to his senses. Working on *Mister Roberts* gave Jack Lemmon a chance to study James Cagney at work, and he says it was one of the great lessons in building up his career.

Jimmy and Bill were waiting for Lemmon when he arrived at Midway. "Tell me," Jimmy asked him when they met. "Are you still using your left hand exclusively when you act?"

At first, the young actor was completely taken aback. Then he remembered that about two years before, he had played in a Kraft television show using only his left hand. He did it purely as an acting discipline. It was not in the script, and he did not think anyone had noticed it. His wife certainly had not. Neither had his agent. But Cagney—that sense of observation as keen as ever—had.

The two men became friends while working on *Mister Rob-*

erts. When they were on the U.S.S. *Hewell* filming the on-board shots, Jimmy taught Lemmon to do a few steps between lunch sandwiches in one of the cabins. When they were on land, during the evenings, they hoofed in the officers' quarters where both were staying.

Time magazine said: "James Cagney makes his Jack-in-the-Box appearance with all of the peppery rancor of a Mr. Punch. The best evidence of the film's accomplishment is that Mister Roberts seldom drags during its more than two hours' running time."

It is fair to say that Jimmy was in the same sort of spirits as he had exhibited when he made *Yankee Doodle Dandy*. It was appropriate that he should have been—for, in his last film of 1955, his fourth that year, he was playing George M. Cohan again.

In the Paramount picture, *The Seven Little Foys*, he joined Bob Hope for a single scene. On top of the table at the New York Friars Club, Cagney as Cohan and Hope as Foy dance to the music of "Yankee Doodle Dandy." They also sang the song "Mary's a Grand Old Name," but the vocal performances were cut from the final print.

The few minutes they were on together, however, had a classic beauty and must rate as among the important moments in the history of the film musical. Jimmy loved the chance to dance again, and Bob Hope, in the first straight role of his career, appreciated the chance of having Jimmy spend a fortnight teaching him to be a "hoofer."

At the end of the two week's work, Cagney refused to take a fee. He said it had been a labor of love. "Any part as George M. Cohan is worth the effort," he explained. Bob Hope and producer Jack Rose, however, thought that Jimmy ought to get some kind of reward. It arrived at his Coldwater Canyon home in the shape of a red-leather-lined horse trailer. Engraved on it was this inscription: "Thanks for the trailer you did for us. Here's one for you."

When he was asked why he had worked so hard in the past few months, he answered: "Looked as if the studios thought they might be fun, that's why. It was no effort. Not for this Irishman."

His other interests were, however, still as keen as ever. And nothing was dearer to his heart than the movement which today is called ecology. In 1955, he was guest of honor at Rollins College in Winter Park, Florida. As he walked to the stage to talk to the undergraduates, they all expected a lecture on Hollywood and the place of the film industry in the nation's economy. Instead, he told them, "I'm hipped on conservation," and went on to talk about the dangers of taking too much out of the earth. He spoke of the "unfilled need of rapidly increasing numbers of people for the essentials of life."

He had never forgotten the lecture he had heard as a small boy in Yorkville and now he had an opportunity to pass on the important message to a new generation of youngsters. Conservation of the soil was a subject he knew very well by now. At about the same time, the Massachusetts Department of Agriculture presented him with a special award for conservation work on his own farm at Martha's Vineyard. When there was talk about building an airport on the Vineyard, Jimmy was in the forefront of the campaign to get it stopped.

In show business, he adopted the conservative approach. He liked his new role on the Hollywood scene—playing only the parts that really appealed to him, whether they made money or not. But he didn't want to do any television.

"TV?" he asked scornfully when the issue was raised by a reporter. "Look. I'm a happy man. Why should I want to look for trouble?"

By 1955 he had made only one television appearance, on a

This Is Your Life show when director William Wellman was guest of honor. "But never again," he said, and explained: "I'm not dependable. There I was, waiting my turn and watching the show on a set in the next room and Bill's eighty-five-year-old mother comes on. Now, I'd already met her. I knew she and Bill were going to be hugging and kissing in front of 25 million people—yet all of a sudden I felt that familiar tugging right here." He pointed to his heart. "And there I was, bawling out loud. Crying like a baby." As he said, "Can't help it. I'm an Irishman. Enjoy nothing better than a good cry. What are you going to do with us?"

He was feeling no more enthusiastic about any brand of show business and just wanted to be left alone on one of the farms—of which there were now four, two in California, the one in New York, and the original at the Vineyard.

"Show business," he declared, "is as unpredictable as a bicycle in heavy traffic. A young kid comes along, does a couple of radio shows, works for a spell with a stock company, does a small bit on the stage. Then he gets a part with which he can do something—and away he goes.

"Everyone asks him: 'Where have you been?'

"To which he should reply: 'I've been in your casting offices, right under your noses all the time—trying to make a lousy buck. Where have you been?'"

James Cagney could never forget what it was like to be waiting. He didn't see anybody waiting to be recognized on a farm, and although there was little money in it, he could see a greater sense of satisfaction in the agricultural life. He took all the agricultural journals and when he came across an item in one of them, he followed it through. He wrote to agricultural engineer Hans Lederman in the small English town of Spaxton, Somerset: "Please let me have the tractor you advertised in a journal that has reached me. Also, a skip loader attachment. I will pay for both from my sterling account in England." The total cost of the tractor and the attachment he wanted to buy was in the region of $1500.

Mr. Lederman was happy to oblige. Unfortunately, the Bank of England was not. They said he could either pay for the tractor in dollars or he could not have it. That went for the skip loader, too.

The British Board of Trade said that the Anglo-American Film Agreement did not permit goods to leave the country and be paid for in sterling. Only dollars would be acceptable. If Jimmy had his own way, he would be using "blocked funds." One American newspaper summed up the predicament: "Cagney loses to Queen."

But Cagney did not want a row. "I suppose the rules are rigid," he conceded and wrote to Mr. Lederman: "I tried to buy some Scottish Highland cattle some time back. No luck. Thanks for the efforts."

Over the years Jimmy had been slowly developing the gifts that were so apparent when he was drawing caricatures of his classmates in his schoolbooks. He still did lightning sketches of people around him using whatever paper was at hand, a large envelope or a sheet of cardboard that had come with the laundry.

In 1956, he had an opportunity to develop that ability to draw as highly as he had developed his talents to perform in a pair of dancing shoes or sit behind the wheel of a tractor. Jack Bailey, emcee of the record-breaking TV show *Queen for a Day*, took Jimmy along to meet a "mad Russian"—a friendly tag for a delightful, tall man called Serge Bongart, who has been living in the United States for about thirty years but still speaks as though he has just brushed the snow of the steppes from his boots.

Bongart is an exceptionally talented painter who has an

equally evident talent for teaching others. He runs his own art school, which is attended by several VIP students. Jack Bailey was one of them.

The idea of introducing Cagney to his teacher came to Bailey when they were lunching together at the famous Brown Derby restaurant in Beverly Hills. They were sitting opposite a youngster whom Jimmy described as a "born cartoon." Cagney sketched him on a table napkin.

The next day, Bailey was at Jimmy's front door and asking him to come for a ride—"to meet my teacher." On the journey, they talked first about Jeanne Cagney, who was a fashion commentator on the *Queen* show, and then about painting. When they arrived at Bongart's home, the painter gave them the warmest possible greeting, and invited the pair in for lunch. He had cooked it himself—Boeuf Stroganoff, washed down by the best vodka. Over the meal, both men talked about their origins. When Jimmy touched on Yorkville and the East Side, he acted out the parts of the youngsters among whom he lived—adding a touch of Yiddish dialect here, a snatch of Italian there. When Bongart revealed that he had fled from the Ukraine, Jimmy topped the story by quoting an obscure Ukrainian proverb in a perfect Ukrainian accent: "Do not say 'hop,'" Jimmy recited, "until you know what you will find on the other side." To this day, Bongart does not know how Cagney knew a proverb few Ukrainians ever used.

The two men had a common denominator that seemed to go beyond their mutual admiration for the work of Pushkin. Bongart says that Cagney's own verse typifies Pushkin's belief that the ideal poem should "contain little space for words, but a great deal of space for thought." As a result of that first meeting, Jimmy began taking regular lessons with Bongart—sometimes visiting his summer retreat in Idaho, where he has a painting school, sometimes his studio in Santa Monica.

It was Cagney's innate sense of artistic good taste which first struck the Russian. Bongart had visited an exhibition by an English landscape painter and then commended his work to Jimmy. Three or four days later, Jimmy proudly showed his teacher three pictures he had bought at the show. "The unbelievable thing," says Bongart today, "is that he chose the three best pictures in the whole exhibition."

Film critics, meanwhile, were commending the more conventional type of picture connected with Cagney. In London, all four films which he made in 1955 opened in the same week. The London *Daily Express* proclaimed: "This is going to be the year of James Cagney. There is nothing more rewarding than seeing an old master swinging back in championship style form." And why was it Cagney's year? "Because he has a vitality that makes the youngsters seem tired."

MGM, meanwhile, had asked Jimmy to return to their fold after the happy relationship between them making *Love Me or Leave Me*. They wanted him to step into the place vacated by Spencer Tracy in a Western called *Tribute to a Bad Man*. Tracy had had a row with the MGM production department and decided he wanted nothing to do with their film. Cagney saw that it offered the opportunity for his own kind of characterization and took it.

Tribute to a Bad Man was not a good film and neither, really, was the role he played of a ruthless but appreciative ranch owner in the midst of a horse-raiding war. But he saw the possibilities and he exploited them. There were some magnificent scenic shots and it was no less a joy watching Cagney recite his lines on the back of a horse in this film than it had ever been. One cannot help thinking Jimmy did the film simply because of all the horses. As *The New York Times* remarked: "Any way you look at it, the old master James Cagney really is at home in *Tribute to a Bad Man*."

Making his next film, Cagney was more at home out of

camera range than he was within it. He and Barbara Stanwyck were making *These Wilder Years,* the story of a man's search for his twenty-year-old illegitimate son. Cagney was the man; Barbara Stanwyck, the head of the home from which the boy had been sent for adoption. The screenplay was mainly the confrontation between the two—he, explaining he regretted disowning the boy; she warning that she would go all the way to court to prevent him making contact with him. In the end, he does the "right" thing and adopts a teen-age unmarried mother to give her and her baby a proper start.

The movie did not really do justice to either of the stars. But when the lights were turned off and the camera was stopped, they made up for the inadequacies of the film and danced the Charleston together. They had both begun their professional careers as hoofers, and both had also been discovered by Al Jolson—Jimmy in *Penny Arcade* and Barbara when, as a girl named Ruby Stevens, she had won a Charleston contest that Jolson was judging. But if they enjoyed being together, it did not seem obvious when the film was completed. The New York *World Telegram* described their performances as "competently troubled."

He was no longer troubled about his career, however. Louis Sobel, writing for the New York *Journal American,* wondered if he would contemplate returning to the Broadway stage. "Never entered my mind," he told him. "I'm too wrapped up in pictures. It answers all my urges. Besides, I might be a bit scared."

Meanwhile, the younger James Cagney, who had been kept out of the limelight throughout his life to date, decided he was going to keep it that way. He had no urges for any kind of show business, he said. But he did share his adoptive father's love of the soil, and he was going off to Cornell University to study farming. One wag said he "preferred ham on the hoof to ham on the screen."

His father, though, now agreed that the time had perhaps

come to start thinking more seriously about the smaller screen. He rang his friend Robert Montgomery and said he was willing to keep the promise he had made after *The West Point Story*—to cash in the rain check to work in one of his television plays. The play he agreed to do was *Soldier from the Wars Returning,* a story by Robert Wallace about an Army sergeant assigned to escort home for burial the body of a Korean War hero.

At Eaves, the theatrical costumier's, the tailor measuring Jimmy for his sergeant's uniform noticed that his waist measurement was identical to the one he had last taken from him years before. He wanted to know the secret. "Just dancing," Jimmy told him. And he pointed out the little canvas bag which he took along on all rehearsals. It contained his dancing shoes.

When the uniform was ready to be worn in the play, a studio executive apologized for the demotion being inflicted on Cagney following his role as the captain in *Mister Roberts.* Jimmy said he was resigned to it. "That's the history of this business!" he joked.

He said, however, that he had no intention of starting a new career in television. "I do enough work in the movies. This is a high-tension business." But he had "tremendous admiration for the people who go through this sort of thing week after week." He had seen a television comedian having so much trouble with his lines that he felt deeply sorry for him. There was a knot in his own stomach as he watched the man trying to fight what had now become a serious attack of nerves. He did not think he would like to have to go through that. But he liked watching television—provided any of his own films were not showing. If they were, he would either switch the set off or go for a walk.

One of the most frequently televised Cagney films these days is also one of the best. *Man of a Thousand Faces,* made for Universal International in 1957, was the first biographical movie in which he had had the leading role since *Yankee Doodle Dandy* sixteen years earlier. This time he was interpreting the "troubled life" of Lon Chaney, Sr., and doing so with great dignity. Chaney was a star of the silent screen, so there was no music, no chance to do any hoofing, and little of the fun of the earlier picture. But there was Cagney's usual grace, intelligence, and sincerity.

Chaney was the man who had virtually invented the horror movie. At the same time, he was the supreme master of the art of makeup, who nevertheless took with him to his grave in 1930 the secrets that had always baffled his contemporaries. They did know, however, that when he played the Hunchback of Notre Dame, he used to throw his shoulder out of joint to get the right effect. Reliving that performance, Cagney contented himself with seventy-two pounds of makeup, including the most vicious-looking leather straps.

Jimmy said the film gave him "great satisfaction." He could sympathize with Chaney without having to identify with him. "He was a man with his own instinctive pattern of living," he explained. But the real satisfaction was in "trying to give today's youngsters an impression of one of the great men of the early movies."

He gave an enchanting performance right from the start of the film, when he cries beneath his clown's makeup. It was a real-life Pagliaccio performance that had actually happened. Chaney's parents are deaf mutes, but his wife (Dorothy Malone) can only think that he will transmit their misfortune to her own child. She resents the sign language he uses for prayer, although he tells her that is the only way he can make those prayers mean anything. As he dies of cancer, Cagney makes the death scene as memorable as the gathering around his father's bed had been in *Yankee Doodle Dandy*. The tears flowed as copiously and as spontaneously. There were also moments of magnificent pantomime—particularly where Jimmy impersonates an old lady trying to thread a needle.

People inevitably compared it with *Yankee Doodle Dandy,* and indeed the film did have its similarities. For one, Jeanne was in *Man of a Thousand Faces*—and again playing his sister.

When the film opened in London, the man often described as Chaney's direct successor, Boris Karloff, was at the premiere, and said how deeply moved he had been by the experience. *The New York Times*'s Bosley Crowther said Cagney had done a "superlative job."

Later that same year, 1957, Jimmy took on a completely new role. Apart from a brief appearance in the prologue, he did not appear at all in the next film that had his name emblazoned across the credits. Instead, for *Short Cut to Hell,* he was, for the first time in his life, a film director. It was not an inspiring film, and Robert Ivers in the lead role was the only performer whose name remotely meant anything. But Jimmy was not looking for an opportunity to make a new name for himself. He was simply helping a pal.

A. C. Lyles, a young man of charm and personality, had been producing a number of B pictures—mainly Westerns—for Paramount. He and Jimmy had been firm "buddies." Directing a film for the man he had always called, simply, "A.C." seemed to Jimmy the most natural thing in the world—if that way he could get a start in major production. He did not try to throw his weight around. When he first moved onto the set, he told the cameraman, "You put the damn box [the camera] where it ought to be."

Cagney took only a "tiny" fee for the job, but agreed he would have a share of the profits. How much these profits have been is a matter for guesswork. He certainly made no fortune from this foray into directing. A. C. Lyles, on the other hand, has to this day remained deeply grateful. Jimmy, though, says he never wants to do it again: "I've no desire to tell other people their business," he said afterward. "My point of view is you hire a man because he knows his stuff."

To Jimmy, directing *Short Cut to Hell* was no act of charity. It was the same when he saw a painting by a young artist. He would buy it not because he needed the picture but because he thought he might give a youngster a break. When he heard a young man had gone without decent food for a couple of days, he rang a restaurant and told the owner: "Feed this boy—till he gets a job." The restaurant did feed him and Jimmy paid the bills, until the boy found a job with prospects.

The 1958 film *Never Steal Anything Small* was a sort of musical. It gave him the chance to dance a bit and sing a little, but it was neither a *Yankee Doodle Dandy* nor—fortunately—a *West Point Story*. The film was about a waterfront union battle and, out of nowhere, Jimmy would stand on a truck and sing. Essentially, it was one of his old tough-guy roles with the addition of the music. It was an amusing couple of hours, but little more. In some ways, the story line resembled *Guys and Dolls,* but the music did not.

His next picture the following year saw Cagney going back to his Irish roots. It was also the only film he ever made in Ireland. *Shake Hands with the Devil* was about the first wave of Irish troubles this century—the ones leading up to the setting up of the Irish Free State. Cagney was so good in this film that he even overshadowed players of the caliber of Sir Michael Redgrave and Dame Sybil Thorndike. Jimmy would probably never regard that as a compliment. He would be afraid it conjured up notions of his trying to steal a scene.

He played a doctor who was also an IRA commandant. *Time* magazine was to say it was an "everyday Irish stew of a picture." But it was an unfair judgment on a film in which Jimmy stood out as a giant. *The New York Times* was much nearer the mark in describing it as "one of the fastest, toughest, and most picturesque dramas about the Irish revolution." The London *Evening Standard* said Jimmy gave "one of the most memorable performances" in the picture. It certainly seemed that way to the Irish people who watched the filming and became very much part of the whole operation.

In Ireland, Cagney was treated not just as a visiting celebrity, but as a local boy made good. The fact that his links with Ireland had been confined to Irish New York made little difference. But when he was given a full celebrity reception, Jimmy was plainly disturbed.

"Twenty years ago, I might have rated the big-star treatment," he said, "but not now." And as if to demonstrate just how out of touch he was with the life of a big star, he walked around in a pair of old carpet slippers. The image was somewhat spoiled, however, when it was revealed that the slippers had cost about a hundred dollars.

Jimmy was also conscious of his age. He was already sixty years old, his waist was beginning to put on inches, and he was slightly deaf. But as if to show he could still do a jig as well as anyone else, he gave something of a press conference in a deserted studio, while a technician played on an upright piano.

As his face grew redder and the sweat poured down his face, soaking his bushy eyebrows, he explained why he continued to dance every moment that he was not actually on call: "Gotta" —pause—"too fat. I gotta"—pause again—"lose eight pounds. I gotta get in trim." And, as far as he was concerned, there was no better way than this of doing it.

The Irish jig to which he was hoofing now changed to "Yankee Doodle *Boy*." He was still dancing and talking: "People get the idea"—pause—"that all film actors have to do is walk on to a set, do as they are told, and collect a sum of money. It's not so. It's a job of work like any other job, you gotta be ready."

He worried about always being ready. "I knew a guy who didn't take any exercise at all between pictures. He had to run in one film. Took his heart by surprise." Jimmy pounded his chest as he always would at moments like this and added thoughtfully: "Went phhpht."

For a time, *Shake Hands with the Devil* seemed bedeviled itself, mainly by business worries. Originally, it was to be made by a company headed by Marlon Brando. When people asked him about his association with Brando, Jimmy admitted he had never met him. "Never even seen one of his films. Don't know what Method acting is." And then, only slightly varying the line immortalized a decade later by Frank Sinatra, he added: "I got my own way."

Brando's company bowed out while the film was being shot and was succeeded by young Michael Anderson, then one of the blue-eyed boys of filmmaking. His own company, Troy Films, took over the production. He said he was going to increase the budget by $300,000 to a total of nearly $1.8 million.

Jimmy was happy to fit in with Anderson's plans. He did not interfere with the production now any more than he would have done before, but occasionally he would offer a word of advice. He did not, for instance, like the idea of a props truck constantly blowing gasoline fumes into the faces of actors waiting to go before the camera. "It worries me," he explained. "Knew a fighter once, a very promising boy. Every day for two years he used to train running behind a car. Suddenly, he was taken ill. They thought he'd die. 'Poisoning,' they told him. Two years of breathing exhaust fumes. You've got to be careful of things like that."

The vivid Cagney fund of experience was showing itself once more. He had a heroic aura about him now and the attitude of most people who talked to him was one of hero worship. When a small boy approached him on the Dublin Street where they were filming, he asked: "You want an autograph, Sonny?" And he scribbled his name on a piece of paper. The boy turned up his nose and screwed up the paper.

"Not good enough?" Jimmy asked. "Well, let's try again." He did a quick sketch of himself and signed his name a second time.

The boy walked away. "Okay now?" Jimmy asked, looking relieved. But the boy was not satisfied. Not knowing the value of what he held in his hand, he screwed it up yet again and offered Jimmy a gift in return—a dead mouse. Cagney picked it up by its tail and then pushed it down a nearby drain. "It's probably diseased," he said as the boy finally walked away. "Somebody ought to speak to that lad."

The British Film Institute took advantage of Jimmy's stay on their side of the Atlantic to organize a retrospective showing of some of his old films at the prestigious National Film Theatre. Bill sat with him at the back of the auditorium, occasionally dabbing her eyes with her handkerchief. It was the first time she had seen some of them. People wanted to know whether Jimmy was a tough guy at home. She repeated her favorite phrase: "Oh, he's just a real softie."

The Manchester *Guardian* enjoyed the lecture that Cagney gave after the film show. "A professional of professionals," they called him. "Tough, bouncy on the screen, he showed quiet common sense and an entire lack of histrionic affectation in coping with a bombardment of questions from the audience," they reported.

What people seemed to want to know most was Jimmy's view on the Method, which was still very much in vogue. "Not guilty," he replied. And that was how he felt about seeing his old films most of the time: "Once you've finished a job, you've done with it." But he was making the British Film Institute's tribute an exception.

Bill, however, liked talking about the pictures. Asked about

White Heat, she said: "That's where he gets burned to death. You know, he died dozens of different times. In every picture, I'm a widow."

The Dorothy Parker of Coldwater Canyon was in rare form. "You know, we've stayed married for so long that I think I'm going to charge folks a dollar a time to come and look at us. I try not to order Jimmy about. He's a sentimental Irishman."

At a luncheon at the Guards Club, Jimmy was asked how he would view having his own life story filmed. He said he would not like it. Any Cagney "biopic" would have to be a horror film. "Horribly dull," he added in explanation, lest anyone think he ever was as tough as his image.

When he was asked what he thought about the Cagney films showing at the National Film Theatre, he replied in one word: "Ham." But he added that he would jump at the chance to make another *Yankee Doodle Dandy*. He explained: "There just haven't been others like George M." And possibly that was why *Man of a Thousand Faces* had not succeeded in the way the earlier film had done. But the film he really was pleased with was *Shake Hands with the Devil.* And Michael Anderson? "He's the sort of director I'm right at home with. Knows exactly what he wants—no time wasted."

Jimmy was equally at home with the cast of *Shake Hands with the Devil.* To the juvenile lead, Don Murray, he offered the same sort of paternal protection which he had afforded to Jack Lemmon in *Mister Roberts.* He taught him to dance, too. When Murray's father came on the set to have a look around, Jimmy took him off for a hoofing lesson as well.

At times, it seemed that people in Dublin were taking the filming a little too seriously, however. The film company put an advertisement in the local papers, warning people that there would be explosions and mock machine-gun fire in the streets and asking them not to be alarmed. But as soon as the firing started, local people threw sticks and stones at the actors—obviously believing that the "Troubles" had broken out once more, ten years before they actually did.

Back home again at Martha's Vineyard, Jimmy and Bill walked into an altogether different and more unexpected row. A group of his neighbors complained that he had been using the island for personal publicity purposes—which perhaps showed just how much the Cagneys had kept to themselves. Had they been more gregarious the locals would have known just how far from a publicity seeker he was. But he did not want to upset anyone. He asked all the newspaper people he knew and the studio publicists, too, to kindly refrain from in any way linking his name with the island. "No mention of an island, initials MV or anything like that in connection with me. Never."

He had decided that the time had arrived for taking a long look at himself. He was breeding Morgan horses, which were ideal for pulling carriages and work purposes, and beef cattle. But he decided he had to keep away from dairy farming. When he had gone into the costings, he discovered he could afford to sell his produce a lot cheaper than could any of the others in the business. He had the money from his films to subsidize his milk, and he thought that was totally unfair to the men who had to make their living in a dairy farm. "It just isn't cricket," he declared, and gave notice there would be no more dairy goods from him.

He was really thinking that the time had come to retire and become a professional farmer. But when he looked at the books he was forced to the inescapable conclusion that the money from the films made farming much easier and less worrying. That did not mean, however, that he felt he ought to do too much on the screen—as another actor at the beginning of the fifties had done.

"That guy would finish one good picture and then not know

what to do with himself. So he'd go to work again. Anything just so he could work. Inevitably, the next picture wouldn't be so good. The one after that would be worse. Then he made a bad one. And he wasn't wanted any more. A lot of actors are like that today. They are greedy. They like money. Pretty soon no one likes them."

But Jimmy did have an idea up his sleeve. He wanted to play the part of Fleet Admiral William F. Halsey in a biographical picture. Halsey was the commander of the U.S. Third Fleet in the Pacific and had become known as a man of integrity while shooting down a total of 911 Japanese aircraft, destroying 71 ships, and damaging another 92. "You can imagine what a fanciful character he'd be to play," he mused. He got his wish and the picture was called *The Gallant Hours.*

The film was produced and directed by Jimmy's old friend Robert Montgomery, who was also a Navy Reserve officer. It was not altogether successful. It used the semidocumentary technique of having a constant sound-track commentary and went into such detail that it even included the kind of camera the admiral used to photograph flowers.

The film was also fairly static, with most of the time being spent inside Halsey's cabin and very little footage filmed outside. It opened with Halsey taking leave of his crew as he begins his retirement. The story of the admiral's Pacific war is told in flashback and the movie ends as it began, on the deck of his ship.

But it was the usual story of a Cagney performance far outweighing the value of the film in which he was acting. Halsey was known as "Bull." The way Cagney played him, it was easy to see why. He was a typical Cagney character—warm, humane, concerned, and with a sense of humor—but in uniform. *The New York Times* called it "one of the quietest, most reflective, subtlest jobs that Mr. Cagney has ever done."

He was able to make it such by doing his own research and

in his usual way getting to know his subject. He met Halsey and discovered his underlying compassion. During the war, the admiral had declared his belief that "the only good Jap was a dead one." But that gave a misguided view of the man. When Halsey came to the United Artists studio to see the film being made he told the cast: "It's easy to keep saying 'Attack' when you don't have to carry out the orders yourself. I'll never forget the boys who died." He was too emotional to complete the sentence.

He was asked to pick the actors up on any faults he found with their interpretations, but he refused to do so. Halsey said that was none of his business. "You're the pros." But he did agree to correct Jimmy if he saw any typical Cagney mannerisms seeping through. He could find none. Robert Montgomery was asked to do the same thing, but he found little to fault either.

Cagney described the picture as "a labor of love and gratitude to a man who, when the chips were down, performed for us."

It was also another Cagney family film. James Cagney, Jr., momentarily broke his vow and appeared as an extra. So did Bob Montgomery and his son.

Like George M. Cohan, Admiral Halsey liked the way Cagney portrayed him on the screen. And, like George M. Cohan, he died soon after his life story was completed in 1960.

A year later, Jimmy started work on a totally different kind of film. With a young beauty called Pamela Tiffin and the accomplished actress Arlene Francis he went to Berlin, and there joined up with German actor Horst Buchholz. He was going to play the boss of Coca-Cola's German interests. The cold war was blowing as cold as ever and Berlin was at the center of it all. But so far there was no wall between East and West and it still seemed like the subject for a good joke.

One, Two, Three, the film they made, was a good joke, ably supported by director Billy Wilder and his collaborator I. A. L. Diamond. It turned out to be quite the funniest, most offbeat picture Jimmy ever made.

He played not just the head of the Coca-Cola operation but also the man forced to become the guardian of the company president's daughter (Pamela Tiffin). This mink-wearing girl from Alabama falls for a young Communist and Cagney has to find a way of turning him into a capitalist. He does it by dressing his own Prussian assistant as a woman, and sending the young Red into the Eastern Zone with a balloon bearing the legend "Ruskies go home" attached to the exhaust pipe of his motorcycle.

Pamela Tiffin's name in the picture is Scarlett. At one point, Cagney asks his wife (Arlene Francis), "I wonder what happened to Scarlett?" She replies: "Probably gone with the wind."

The young Miss Tiffin was very nervous at the prospect of working with Cagney. He therefore decided it was his duty to try to put her at ease. For her, he went through a potpourri of his old roles—and showed how he could imitate his imitators, hitching his trousers with his wrists.

"Sometimes I wonder if they're kidding me or Edward G. Robinson," he laughed, and everyone laughed with him. Pamela was able to act a lot better after one of those sessions —especially when he revealed that he had only met Clark Gable once and Gary Cooper four times.

Jimmy took advantage of the breaks between shooting to do what he wanted to do most of all, have a look at the countryside where he was working. One day, he and some friends were driving in the French-German border area near the banks of the Rhine. They were anxiously looking for a bridge that would take them across the water. Finally, they saw coming toward them what they took to be a typical French peasant—complete with Clemenceau mustache, cap, and corduroy trousers.

Cagney's driver spoke to him in French, but the man was

not able to understand. Jimmy heard him muttering to himself in German.

"Si kennan Deutsch sprachen?" Jimmy asked—and then saw the stranger couldn't stop himself from laughing.

"Ah," said the man, "Yiddish!"

Jimmy, who flattered himself on his impeccable German, still spoke with the Yiddish accent he had picked up at Stuyvesant High School—and he has never been able to live it down. He has a close friend who speaks perfect high-class German and who cringes every time Jimmy opens his mouth for a conversation in the language.

No one cringed after watching *One, Two, Three*. Only the London *Evening Standard* offered a sour note: "As far as taste is concerned," wrote their critic, *"One, Two, Three* is a film that deserves to be counted out before it gets into the ring."

That was also Cagney's judgment on his own career. It was time to count it out. He was retiring.

20 A MIDSUMMER NIGHT'S DREAM

THE IDEA of retirement finally took root when a postcard arrived from three of his friends. He was putting the final touches to *One, Two, Three* in Hollywood but the photographs on the front of the postcard showed his friends and their wives standing on the deck of Jimmy's boat. On the back they had scribbled the message: "Thank God, you're gainfully employed."

The postcard was handed to him as he sat outside the Goldwyn studios on a bright, sunny day. Just then an assistant director tapped him on the shoulder and said: "We're ready for you, Mr. Cagney."

Jimmy confesses that was the moment he heard himself say: "That's it, baby." There were more important things to do than working under arc lamps when the sun was shining so brightly outside. He had lent his boat to his friends, but now he wanted to start using it himself.

When the news leaked out, it was greeted as a message of abdication. In London, the city which more and more had taken this typical New Yorker to its heart, the *Daily Express* published an editorial of the kind usually reserved for royalty or departing statesmen:

"James Cagney, who is retiring, was the last of the great screen gangsters. He was so successful in that role that real-life gangsters were numbered among his fans.

"Physically, he was insignificant. How then was he so convincingly tough? Physique may hold an audience, talent captivate it. But only one quality has magic. Character."

Now Cagney was determined to start a new life. Friends never thought he would do it and wagered a total of thousands of dollars to say so. He happily took their bets. "I'm an ex-actor," he announced. "That's the kind of business I like. Acting needs enthusiasm and I don't have that enthusiasm now. There'll be no comeback."

Still people did not believe him, so he underlined a few words: "When you've been in the business as long as I have been and you begin to feel uninterested, it's time to quit—get out and stay out. You need enthusiasm for this job. You've got to get up with your blood pounding. I just don't feel like doing it any more."

He did agree that life had been good and "my business has been good to me." But he was making it plain that he didn't want any more of it. Besides, he had financial security and his farms could manage without a film star's subsidy. "I've got enough to see me through," he said. Above all, he was looking forward to working on his farms—"pitchin' in. And I can still dirty my hands if I want to."

He still had no exaggerated ideas about his contribution to society. "In the movies, I went out and did a job. That's all. When directors asked me to do something, I just went ahead and did it. That's what most people do in a lifetime, isn't it? Most actors are no different. They do what they are told."

For Bill it was the end of seeing her husband off to the "office" every morning. That was the perspective Jimmy had taught her to put into their life together. They had taught their children to adopt the same philosophy, and they were both pleased with the results. Marine Corporal James Cagney, Jr., announced that he was going to marry another corporal in the Marines, Jill Inness, and both were pleased to see that there was hardly a ripple of interest thereafter. As for Jimmy himself, he just hoped no one would ask him to pose—as he had been asked a year or so before his retirement—with Mae Clarke and a half grapefruit. All he really wanted to do now was sit back and applaud someone else. He and Bill would take more holidays—and if he wanted to go away for spells with "the boys" that was all right, too.

Jimmy, his brothers Harry and Ed, and Serge Bongart went off to Europe on a cargo boat. The idea of avoiding a more luxurious vessel was so that they could travel without hundreds of people dogging them throughout the voyage. They were going to Spain, but were calling in Egypt on the way. One man said he even recognized Jimmy from the shape of the back of his neck. Around the docks, his Egyptian fans stood in line to shake his hand and pummel him on the back.

When they got to Madrid, the party went to a night club. Jimmy was beginning to feel uncomfortable and suggested they all get up to leave just before the end of the floor show, so that they would not be spotted when the lights came up. Just as they were about to creep out, Jimmy stepped on a cat—and all hell seemed to be let loose as the poor animal screamed. The lights went on and for two hours Jimmy was signing autographs, posing for pictures. At a bullfight, a magazine photographer planted himself next to the supposedly retired actor and took one picture after the other, clicking away as Jimmy joined in the *olé's*.

Above all, that holiday was a chance to paint. Jimmy and his Russian art teacher had one thing in common—they both enjoyed living like bums. The happiest times were when they planted themselves outside a workingmen's cafe, bought a hunk of cheese, a stick of salami, and a loaf of bread and then settled down beside their easels with a bottle of cheap wine to wash down the snack.

With men, women, and children hanging around them, they would get down to the serious business of painting—interrupting brush strokes only to dig a pocket knife into the cheese. As they painted, they talked more about their childhood, with Jimmy once again acting out every part as he went back to the days in Yorkville. Neither ever bothered with small talk. As Bongart says today: "Every word has a meaning—and love and feeling." When the mood took him, Jimmy would show his teacher a dance step that just came to his mind. "I called him the Anna Pavlova of softshoe," the Russian says with an understandable chuckle.

On this trip, the Cagney party linked up with film producer Sam Bronston, who at the time was building a mini-Hollywood in Spain. When Bronston discovered that both he and Bongart hailed from the same Ukrainian city—Kiev—they were like soul brothers. Jimmy for once was the outsider as they talked to each other in their native dialect. Next day, the party joined the film director for lunch. He, in turn, introduced them to his brilliant French cameraman—and a new discovery. He, too, was born in Kiev. "My God," said Jimmy in mock despair. "It makes me sick." He collapsed laughing.

Later in the tour, the party were given a private exhibition by the celebrated picador Ingela Peralto. Jimmy wanted to meet him because he had heard he had a fine collection of horses. Peralto said he had just imported a number of new ones from Russia and asked the artist to translate the documents that accompanied them. To Cagney's professed considerable annoyance, the papers showed that they, too, had come from Kiev.

It was at moments like this that Jimmy would find an appropriate phrase in Yiddish. "It's a whole magillah," he said.

Whenever Cagney returned from a trip, one thing would be certain to be awaiting him: a stack of scripts. All of them would be returned, usually unread, certainly without any intention of taking any of the offers accompanying them.

Only once did he appear to weaken—when Warner Bros. thought he would be ideal cast as the father of Eliza Doolittle in their film version of *My Fair Lady.* Playing the dustman Doolittle was a song-and-dance part and Jimmy had to admit he felt a tug. But he refused to allow it to be more than that. He had to decide for himself if he was still "interested" in show business or not. He knew that at heart he was not interested.

All over the world, Cagney festivals were held and all over the world there were rumors that he was going back to work. He was invited to do a ten-second television commercial for a reputed $180,000, but turned it down. "When I said I was giving up acting, I meant it," he emphasized.

British producer Michael Klinger was reported to have offered him a blank check—certainly one in the region of $1 million. But he turned it down flat. Dorothy Manners, a newspaper columnist, reported that he told her: "Just forget any rumors you may hear that the famous old grapefruit thrower is back in front of the cameras." Nor did the famous old grapefruit thrower see more than a handful of anyone else's films. He had enjoyed *Oliver!*—he said he thought it was "so marvelous." He thought *Patton* was a "very good job" and *1776* made him "cry all the way through—you know us Irish. We cry at card tricks. But, yeh, I loved it."

He was once asked whether he had seen *Last Tango in Paris.*

"Missed that one," he replied.

Just occasionally, he would do some work in a film studio, but he would not act—and that was final. He did not want to do any more directing, either. But he agreed to act as narrator for his friend A. C. Lyles in a Western he produced in 1966 called *Arizona Bushwackers*. He also agreed to be the voice of Smokey the Bear in a Forest Service film called *The Ballad of Smokey the Bear*. In 1973, he did the commentary in a special filmed tribute to Edward G. Robinson shown at the time a posthumous Oscar was presented to his widow.

But for years he did not want any tributes to himself. For the most part, James Cagney drove around in a four-year-old Chevrolet station wagon, wearing a gray suit he had had in his closet for twenty years. His hat looked even older.

On one occasion, Serge Bongart told a neighbor about his friend and talented pupil who always drove the old Chevy. His neighbor asked to meet him. A few minutes later, Jimmy arrived—in a shiny Rolls-Royce.

"What the hell do you think you're doing?" Bongart asked him. "Here I am telling everyone what a modest man you are and you come and see me in a Rolls-Royce."

Cagney looked positively embarrassed. "Oh, hell," he said. "My daughter took the Chevrolet and my wife took her car and I was left with this . . . this monster. I've had it for fifteen years and never drive it."

He always tried to keep a sense of proportion, and driving a Rolls-Royce was not the way he saw himself. All he wanted to do was be himself and keep healthy.

In 1964 his brother Harry died suddenly at the age of sixty-six. Four years later, his younger brother Ed followed him. He was sixty-eight and had had a heart attack.

Jimmy's immediate reaction was to have himself looked over by a doctor. The doctor decided it would be interesting to see why people like Cagney, who used their bodies hard all their lives, appear to have sound hearts. Jimmy agreed to be his guinea pig and found that he passed the physical with flying colors. "You're fine," said the doctor. "But I wouldn't be able to say this if you were a smoker." Jimmy decided not to smoke at all after that.

In 1972, Jimmy and Bill celebrated their golden wedding anniversary, a quiet affair with no pictures in the newspapers. The question of pictures was to become one of Jimmy's sensitive points when he moved from his mid-sixties to his seventies.

A picture of him wearing a gray top hat and sitting in an open horse-drawn carriage was probably responsible for rumors that he was growing dreadfully fat. He had, indeed, put on a fair amount of weight, which was always a family characteristic. But the picture exaggerated the Cagney jowls out of all proportion and embarrassed him.

In fact, so few pictures of Cagney have been published in recent years that when a Florida newspaper showed him in 1972 wearing a white beard, nobody appeared to turn a hair —except, when he heard about it, Jimmy himself.

The caption said that it was a picture of James Cagney, surrounded by a bevy of chorus girls after being made honorary mayor of Hollywood, Florida. The ceremony was accurately reported, with just one exception. James Cagney telephoned the Miami *Herald* from his house on Coldwater Canyon and said that not only had he not been there the previous day, "I haven't been in Florida for a long time. Hell, I don't think I've ever been to Miami." And he added, "I've never had a beard."

The "James Cagney" in the picture turned out to be the guest of a Miami real-estate man. It was a repeat of an old story that had been going the rounds for forty years. People were always claiming to be James Cagney. Once a young man was given a job on the strength of being Jimmy's son. "If they think they're making a living out of it," said Jimmy in 1972, "well, that's okay with me. But this guy in Miami has done some mischief. If I get my hands on the bum, he'd better watch out."

If that bit of mischief did not amuse Jimmy, neither did another late in 1973. The UPI wire service range A. C. Lyles in Hollywood to tell him his old friend was dead. A shocked A. C. immediately rang the Cagney house to talk to Bill and found Jimmy answering the phone himself. As in the case of Mark Twain, the report of his death had been greatly exaggerated.

Jimmy was at home watching the Frank Sinatra comeback performance on television, completely oblivious to the news. Not only was he fit and well but five days later he would be traveling west.

He and Bill still would not fly, so they were going to drive across country at a steady fifty miles an hour. They would have gone by train but the railroad company would not allow them to take their German shepherd, Lady, on the journey. So they were going to ask their driver to take it nice and easy and do the trip from their New York farm in about nine days, hoping to catch some November sunshine on the way.

Jimmy wanted to be in especially good form. He had a date in Los Angeles, at the Century Plaza Hotel, four months later.

21 COME FILL THE CUP

JAMES CAGNEY may never have thought of himself as a Hollywood person, but on the night of March 13, 1974, Hollywood was Cagney's kingdom. The old stars, the old Hollywood glamour that most people thought was dead returned for a night to pay tribute and say thank you to "the feisty little Irishman."

That was how Frank Sinatra referred to the man that night being given the American Film Institute's Life Achievement Award. And by the clapping, the cheering, and the homage being paid by the two thousand people there in the Century Plaza, that was exactly how it seemed James Cagney was to be affectionately immortalized. The goodies sprinkled for a lifetime had come home to roost.

For three months, Jimmy had sat in his home in Coldwater Canyon, sunning himself by the pool and waiting for what would be his first public appearance in thirteen years. When he mounted the rostrum for a press conference the previous January, a slightly shaky voice revealed a nervousness that had never shown itself in sixty-five films. But the press was with him in the way that they had always been. Thousands of reviews had contained but a handful of harsh words about the work of James Cagney, actor. In January 1974, reporters who had come from all over the United States and abroad gave as warm a reception as they knew how to James Cagney, the man.

He was asked if he ever still went to the movies. Jimmy said he did not. Did he go to the theater? He did not. What was the secret of being happily married? "She's been wonderful for fifty-one years. Lucky man!" said Jimmy.

Then he revealed the big secret: "I never said 'You dirty rat!'" He had gotten the American Film Institute to check all his films and no one could find it in any of the sixty-five movies now in the Library of Congress.

Which film made Jimmy feel proudest? He had to tell the truth: "It's not a question of being proud. It's a matter of liking the ones that turned out satisfactorily." And he listed under that heading *Yankee Doodle Dandy, City for Conquest*—"which was one hell of a book"—and *Love Me or Leave Me*.

As for the award, it was being given—as it had been to John Ford the year before—to the "individual whose talent has in a fundamental way contributed to the filmmaking arts, whose accomplishments have been acknowledged by scholars, critics, professional peers, and the general public and whose body of work has stood the test of time."

This definition of James Cagney's work was certainly accepted by the people gathering for the award presentation on March 13 as well as those watching it in their homes on television five days later.

Sinatra recalled the time he approached Jimmy from behind in a restaurant and whispered the words: "Ma's dead!" Cagney had replied: "Francis. That is the worst imitation I have heard in my whole life."

And the man whom Jimmy calls his best imitator, Frank

Gorshin, gave his impression of how Cagney could hitch his trousers, squeeze up his face and yell—all, he suggested, from holding a burning match! With Kirk Douglas and George Segal, he impersonated Cagney impersonating George M. Cohan singing "Give My Regards to Broadway" and added a final phony "dirty rat" for good measure.

Bob Hope told how much he appreciated the training he had received from Jimmy when they did their dance routine together in the Foys film. He said that Cagney's definition of a love scene was "when he lets the other guy live."

Governor Ronald Reagan asked for people to forget his own films, but honor Jimmy, whom he had known "for the better part of my life." And then he added: "The time I've known Jimmy Cagney *has* been the better part of my life."

Other stars came on to say the same sort of thing: Jack Lemmon, Shirley MacLaine, John Wayne, George C. Scott— who refused an Oscar for himself but flew across the continent to pay tribute as "the man who played Patton to the man who played Admiral Halsey." Doris Day said how much she would have loved to have done another *Love Me or Leave Me* with him and the whole vast hotel ballroom darkened to reveal her image on the screen singing "You Made Me Love You." That was, she said, exactly how she felt.

Then James Cagney came to the podium himself, did a little dance, and now officially stated, before millions, that he really had never said "You dirty rat." "What I did say was 'Judy, Judy, Judy' "—and the house collapsed again at his perfect impersonation of Cary Grant.

Jimmy remembered the past, right back to the days in Yorkville. The boys with whom he grew up were, he said, "part of the stimulating environment which produced the unmistakable touch of the gutter—without which this evening would never have happened." He asked all the Cagney impersonators to acknowledge the debt that they undoubtedly owed to the pimp who stood on the corner of Seventy-eighth Street and First Avenue.

For him it was a very emotional moment and he showed it. The voice cracked and there was an Oscar-sized lump in his throat as he accepted the award. "You've got to hang on, boy," he said to himself—and at least 25 million people heard and felt for him.

George Stevens, Jr., the American Film Institute director, said the award was being presented to a man who sang, acted, and machine-gunned his way into our hearts."

Frank Sinatra simply sang a song—special lyrics by Sammy Cahn to the tune of "My Way": "James Cagney is . . . the total whizz . . . he did it his way."

22 JIMMY THE GENT

THE Life Achievement Award can now stand beside his Oscar, and James Cagney can stand by his record. The red hair has turned white. The trim little body does now have a paunch. Yet he is happy to reflect on his impact on generations of filmgoers—and then go out to paint another fence or another canvas.

He long ago made up his quarrel with Jack Warner, who was not well enough to attend the award ceremony for the Professional Againster. Jimmy is satisfied with what he has done without ever wanting to do it again.

His family and friends were amazed that he agreed to accept the Life Achievement Award and be forced to listen to tributes to himself. He says he did so only because he appreciated the value of an organization like the American Film Institute, which wanted to help train young American filmmakers. He was delighted that on the night of the award presentation, three scholarships were also being presented to young people entering the industry.

At all his homes, the scripts continue to pile up and he continues to turn them down. He is a gentle man. His friends and the few strangers who visit with him by prior arrangement are given a kind, warm welcome. But he is just as likely to have an off-duty stunt man acting as his bodyguard to keep out the unwelcome callers.

He laughs a lot and falls back on the idiom of the East Side if the mood takes him. If he talks to a woman on the phone, he can say: "Hello, goil." His "goil" Bill remains the most important factor in his life—together with their married children and their four grandchildren.

The night the presentation was made, his sister Jeanne sat at his table, proudly wiping away the tears. But his brother Bill, who became one of the most successful real-estate men in Southern California, was too ill to attend.

Jimmy, meanwhile, continues to keep in shape by swimming regularly in his pool and by "hoofing" around the place, wherever he is. He has given up judo because he thought it was too much to ask of a man with a size eighteen collar.

Every year he goes for his regular physical checkup in Los Angeles and he immediately phones one of his close friends—Ralph Bellamy, Pat O'Brien, or any other surviving member of the "Irish Mafia"—with the news that he has been given a clean bill of health.

When people he knows have family celebrations, he is the first to be invited. When they have tragedies, he is the first to be told. When Frank McHugh's son was killed, Jimmy raced to his side to give a close friend's comfort.

He still professes never to see his old films. But when he is with friends and one of the movies is coming up on television, he will usually weaken sufficiently to agree to watch it in their company. Generally, he protests that he hates the experience.

But when *Yankee Doodle Dandy* was showing, A. C. Lyles, sitting next to him, felt a kick on the shin. Jimmy was going through the old dance routines without moving from his chair.

His farms on Martha's Vineyard and in Dutchess County are still his real passions. He breeds whiteface cattle and Morgan horses and grows the corn and hay he needs to feed them. The days, he says, are still not long enough for all he wants to do on the land. His winters are spent in California, either at the Coldwater Canyon house or another home he now has at Twentynine Palms in the desert near Palm Springs—a city which he insists would be much too sophisticated for him.

In the desert, he and Ralph Bellamy sit together, sometimes reminiscing over old times, often saying nothing at all. Their political views are "diametrically opposed," says Bellamy, but they could not feel closer. No one would today have the effrontery to raise a Red scare about James Cagney, and a few years back, he was in the vanguard of the Hollywood campaign for Ronald Reagan's election to the California governorship.

But Jimmy does worry about the corruption of moral life in the 1970's. He likes to tell the story of two policemen—one getting old and with a fraying uniform; the other, young and proud of the graft which has made him rich. The young cop looks at the older man's coat and sneers that honesty did not appear to have gotten him very far. "Right," said the old man. "I've got just two nickels to rub together. But I want to tell you, you son of a bitch, that there isn't one drop of whore's sweat on either of them."

Life to James Cagney is full of morals. History is full of lessons. That is why he reads one book about the Civil War after the other. He has a voracious appetite for reading, often waking up in the middle of the night to continue a new biography that fascinates him. Recently, he read a life of Whistler—and again, he admits, came something of the old tug. "I thought to myself, Ah, if I were twenty years younger that's the film I should have liked to make. But . . . too late."

It is, however, never too late for the other things in his life. His painting has gotten better over the years, and recently Johnny Carson bought a still-life painted on a piece of old shirt cardboard for $5500. It went to SHARE, a charity for specially gifted children. When Jimmy heard about that he said: "My God, I hope he can write it off." He describes his work as "strictly union—in the old days of vaudeville you would hand out your music. Some guys would go with you where you led, but others would only play exactly the notes on the paper. We called those guys 'strictly union.' I paint in a traditional, conventional manner."

He has been offered as much as $15,000 for the rights to reproduce his work. But he won't sell anything commercially. "How could I face those really good artists who've given their whole lives to it and may still be having a hard time making a living?"

He can spend hours going around the galleries studying the work of other painters. Equally, he can spend hours listening to his friends. He thinks his painting has helped him become a good listener. Serge Bongart says he paints as strongly as he used to act. A portrait of a prize fighter has about it the feel of a Cagney punch, the Russian teacher attests. And he also has his taste, which he is happy to spread around. One of his great loves is the work of Charles Russell, the American sculptor of Indian figures. When he stayed with Bongart recently, he brought a Russell bust with him as a gift. It was worth several thousand dollars. Bongart says of Cagney the painter: "If he gave the time to painting that he gave for his movies, he could have been a top painter. If you are good in one field of art, you are generally good in another. You can't be an artist like him and be a bum. He's a very talented man."

He is also still a modest, unpretentious man. Once, quite by accident, he drove with A. C. Lyles past a piece of property which the younger man stopped to admire. "I wonder who owns that?" Lyles asked. "I do," said Jimmy, almost apologetically.

A restaurateur named Herbie Algermissen, who has a small place near Cagney's New York farm, knows he can expect Jimmy and Bill about three or four times a year. They sit at a corner table and just want a quiet meal.

"When he comes through the door," says Algermissen, "you wouldn't know who he is. I guess that's the way he wants it to be. To most people around here, Cagney is just a name, a guy who lives up on the hill."

And that, of course, is James Cagney, a quiet man living up on the hill, whom only his wife, his family, and close friends know well. With them, he will still spend an evening happily singing the old vaudeville songs, accompanying himself on the piano or his guitar. Occasionally, he still entertains them with his own brand of dancing.

In the right mood, he will enjoy an Irish joke session. He particularly likes the ones about wakes. His favorite is the story of the man who had a hard three-day wake for his wife and then said to his friends: "If you think there's a little more fun in it, I'll keep her another day." The really privileged will hear Jimmy recite his poetry. In almost any conversation, he will talk about his patriotism. For him, the age of Yankee Doodle Dandy has not passed. "I still get letters from kids on the positive side," he says. "They say there should be more flag-waving. People should be proud to be Americans. People should shout, 'Proud, proud, proud.'"

James Cagney is also a man of great perception. Pat O'Brien says of him: "He could tell a phony in a fog." To Ralph Bellamy he is "the most honest, the most loyal friend a man could have."

But how does he see himself? As always a song-and-dance man who believes in spreading a few goodies along the way. "I always had that vaudeville feeling," he says. "When you're on, you're on. You've got fifteen minutes to make it in ... No sitting back."

James Cagney has not sat back since the day he learned to help put groceries on the table in Yorkville. If his mother could see him now, she would be able to study the results of her training all those years ago. And he could be pardoned for shouting: "Made it, Ma. Top of the world!"

INDEX

Abbey Players (Dublin), 118-19
Academy Awards, 168, 172, 207
Academy of Motion Picture Arts and Sciences, 87
Ace of Aces, 71
Adler, Luther, 203
Adolfi, John, 62-63
Advertising campaigns, Cagney and, 104, 235
Ah, Wilderness!, 158
Alderman, Johnny, 208
Algermissen, Herbie, 247
Allen, Gracie, 94, 143
All the King's Men, 205
All Women Have Secrets, 141
Alperson, Edward, 122-23
Ameche, Don, 178
American Federation of Actors, 140
American Film Institute, 240, 242-43; Life Achievement Award, 239-43
Anderson, Maxwell, 36
Anderson, Michael, 223, 225
Angels with Dirty Faces, 131-33, 143, 151
Applegate, Mrs. Neville, 182
Arizona Bushwackers, 236
Arliss, George, 62, 63, 118
Arnaud, Max, 36
Arnold, Edward, 175
Associated Actors and Artists of America, 140

Astaire, Fred, 171, 182, 198
Atkinson, Brooks, 40
Ayres, Lew, 61

Bacon, Lloyd, 91, 92, 97, 110, 113
Bailey, Jack, 214-15
Balcon, Sir Michael, 117, 120, 121
Ballad of Smokey the Bear, The, 236
Barnes, Howard, 129, 149-50, 170-71
Barrie, Mona, 124
Barrymore, Lionel, 187
Barthelmess, Richard, 82
Barton, James, 191
Baumer, Marie, 41
"Beer and Blood," 64
Beery, Wallace, 198
Bellamy, Ralph, 90, 107, 108, 109, 143, 244, 245, 248
Bendix, William, 191
Benny, Jack, 34, 182, 187
Berkeley, Busby, 94
Berlin, Irving, 158, 165, 172
Bernstein, Sidney, 118
Bickford, Charles, 37
Blessed Event, 82
Blonde Crazy, 70
Blondell, Joan, 40-42, 59-60, 67, 70, 77, 88, 91, 94, 96
Blood on the Sun, 186-87

249

250 · INDEX

Bogart, Humphrey, 133, 135, 136, 144, 150, 182, 188
Boland, Mary, 39
Bond, Ward, 203
Bongart, Serge, 214-16, 233-34, 236, 246-247
Bowery Boys, 132
Boyer, Charles, 187
Boy Meets Girl, 129-30
"Boys' Club," 108, 119
Brando, Marlon, 154, 223
Breen, Max, 123
Brian, Mary, 90
Bride Came C.O.D., The, 155-56
Bright, John, 64, 65, 70, 77
British Board of Film Censors, 69
British Film Institute, 224
Broadway, 38
Brodkin, Jake, 16
Bronston, Sam, 234
Brown, Joe E., 82, 110-11
Buchholz, Horst, 228
Burns, George, 94

Cagné School of Dancing, 39
Cagney, Bill (Mrs. James Cagney), 31, 33, 35, 38, 39, 40, 83, 85, 87-88, 90, 99, 108-9, 121, 127, 139, 146, 155, 179, 210, 224-25, 233, 237, 244
Cagney, Carolyn Nelson ("Carrie") (mother), 11, 12, 17, 18, 20, 23, 24, 25, 29-30, 31, 86, 109, 140, 141, 155, 185
Cagney, Casey (daughter), 155
Cagney, Edward (brother), 12, 23, 25, 81, 140, 155, 176-77, 205, 233, 236
Cagney, Harry (brother), 12, 18, 23, 24, 25, 81, 155, 176-77, 233, 236
Cagney, James Francis, Jr.: on acting, 40, 71, 73, 82, 116, 167-68, 184, 209, 222, 223, 224, 227, 232; awards received by, 133-34, 168, 174, 239-43; and baseball, 22, 26; birth and childhood of, 12-27; and boxing, 20, 25, 77-78, 152-53; as a celebrity, 72, 109, 222; children of, 155, 178-79, 244; as a comedian, 89, 130, 185, 229, 247; compassion of, 100, 102, 144, 147, 175, 221; and conservation, 17-18, 212; and dancing, 29, 30, 32, 33-34, 39, 94, 124, 184, 202, 211, 218; "death" of, 130-31, 238; as a director, 220-21; early ambitions of, 16, 21-22, 24, 87; earnings of, 34, 60, 64, 70, 73, 78, 127, 136, 142, 174, 190; family ties, 155; and farming, 15-16, 24, 116, 178, 209, 226, 245; and flying, 90, 146, 183, 238; formal education of, 19, 24; health of, 89, 222, 236-37, 244; homes of, 116-17, 138-40, 199, 213, 245; impersonators of, 132, 161, 197, 229, 240-41; and judo, 200, 244; lifestyle of, 61, 85, 88, 107, 109, 121, 127, 149, 179, 244, 245-47; lifetime motto of, 35, 136, 248; marriage of, 31, 108-9, 237, 240; as a narrator, 236; and painting, 215, 234, 246-47; patriotism of, 101, 102, 144, 179, 247; and poetry, 196, 215, 247; and politics, 146, 187-88, 245; professionalism of, 62, 76, 91, 129, 133, 191, 224; retirement of, 231-238; and riding, 131, 134-35, 182, 216; and sailing, 190, 199, 204; sense of observation, 14-15, 16, 21, 29, 35, 128, 210; on show business, 40, 84, 85, 93, 134, 172, 213, 218, 232; show business debut of, 23; as song-and-dance man, 29-35, 39, 94-95, 167, 248 (See also *Yankee Doodle Dandy*); theater work of, 36-42; trademarks of, 61, 63; tributes to, 224, 239-43; and vaudeville, 27-35, 39, 59, 83, 185, 248; voice of, 63, 75, 161; during World War II, 144, 174-75, 178, 179-88
Cagney, James Francis, Sr. (father), 11, 12-13, 17, 20, 22, 24, 74
Cagney, James, Jr. (son), 155, 217, 228, 233
Cagney, Jeanne (sister), 26, 86, 128-29, 140-41, 162, 164, 174, 191, 204, 205, 215, 220, 244
Cagney, William (Bill) (brother), 12, 22, 25, 31-32, 34, 70-71, 94-95, 96, 117, 118, 145-46, 155, 157-58, 160, 162, 166, 167, 173, 176, 177, 179, 190, 192-93, 203, 204, 205, 244
Cagney Circuit, 34
Cahn, Sammy, 242
Calvet, Corinne, 204
Capra, Frank, 87
Captains of the Clouds, 156
Carey, Patrick, 180
Carson, Jack, 154-55
Carson, Johnny, 246
Caught in the Rain, 30
Ceiling Zero, 113-14, 119, 143
Censors. *See* Movie censors
Champlin, Charles, 197
Chaney, Lon, Sr., 219, 220
Chaplin, Charlie, 83, 173

INDEX · 251

Churchill, Winston, 198
City for Conquest, 152-54, 240
Clark, Forrest, 75
Clark, Foster, 130
Clarke, Mae, 67-68, 95, 233
Cohan, Agnes (Mrs. George M.), 165, 166-67
Cohan, George M., 36, 96, 158-70, 172, 211, 225, 228, 241
Coldwater Canyon, home at, 138-40, 180, 239, 245
Come Fill the Cup, 203
Communism, attempts to link Cagney with, 98-102, 125, 144-47, 171
Cooper, Gary, 142, 172, 178, 187, 204, 229
Costello, John M., 125
Crawford, Broderick, 191, 205
Crosby, Bing, 178, 182, 187
Crowd Roars, The, 77, 79
Crowther, Bosley, 68, 170, 198, 202, 205, 206, 220
Curtis, Jack, 159
Curtiz, Michael, 95, 133, 153, 156, 162, 164

Dailey, Dan, 204
Daily Express, London, 75-76, 135, 148, 216, 231-32
Daily Herald, London, 198
Daily Mail, London, 114, 133
Daily Mirror, London, 171
Daily News, New York, 76, 90, 147
Daily Telegraph, London, 121, 137
"Dandy Doodling Yankee, A," 168-69
Davis, Bette, 95, 155-56, 174, 182, 188
Daw, Evelyn, 124
Day, Doris, 202, 204, 207-9, 241
Dead End Kids, 131-32
De Camp, Rosemary, 161
Decker, Caroline, 98-99, 100
De Havilland, Olivia, 111, 155, 188
Delehanty, Thornton, 114
Del Rio, Dolores, 101
Delza, Sophia, 39
Depression, economic, 82, 85
Desire Under the Elms, 36
Devil Dogs of the Air, 104
Diamond, I. A. L., 229
Dies, Martin, 146-47
Dietrich, Marlene, 81
Dillinger, John, 136
Disney, Walt, 187
Dixon, Campbell, 121

Donnelly, Ruth, 90
Doorway to Hell, 61, 65
"Dot's My Boy," 32
Douglas, Kirk, 241
Dunn, James, 71
Durbin, Deanna, 188
Dutchess County, farm in, 199, 245, 247
Dvorak, Anne, 86, 106

Each Dawn I Die, 147-49
Edelman, Louis F., 105, 202
Ellis, Patricia, 104
Elmer the Great, 161
Enemy of the Public (England), 69
England: and Cagney's movies, 69, 77, 89, 123, 133, 138, 171-72, 183, 198; Cagney's trip to, during World War II, 182-85
Epstein, Julius, 162
Epstein, Philip, 162
Etting, Ruth, 208, 209
Evening Journal, New York, 40
Evening Post, New York, 114
Evening Standard, London, 171, 183, 222, 230
Every Sailor, 28-30

Fairbanks, Douglas, 83, 173
Farmingdale School of Agriculture, 18, 24
Fawn, The, 23
Faye, Alice, 143
Field, Lew, 32
Fighting 69th, The, 150-52
Flynn, Errol, 125, 153, 189
Fonda, Henry, 210
Footlight Parade, 94-95
Ford, John, 204, 240
Foy, Eddie, 165, 211
Foy, Eddie, Jr., 107, 165
Francis, Arlene, 228, 229
Francis, Kay, 136
Frank, George, 84
Friars Club, 20, 211
Frisco Kid, 113

Gable, Clark, 71, 76, 127, 174, 198, 229
Gallant Hours, The, 227-28
Garbo, Greta, 149, 198
Garfield, John, 178
Garson, Greer, 172
Gaumont British, 117
George, Gladys, 150
George, Grace, 176

252 · INDEX

Gibbons, Mrs. Douglas, 169
Gibson, Wynne, 32
Glasmon, Kubee, 64, 65, 70, 77
Gleason, James, 203
G Men, 105-6
Goff, Ivan, 194
Goldwyn, Sam, 84
Gorcey, Leo, 132
Gordon, Mary, 109-110
Gorshin, Frank, 240-41
Grand National Pictures Corporation, 122, 123-24, 125, 129
Grand Street Follies, 39
Grant, Cary, 175, 241
Grapefruit Scene from *The Public Enemy,* 67-68
Gray, Joey, 152-53
Great Guy, 122, 123-24
Gribbon, Henry, 33

Hall, Mordaunt, 61, 69, 95
Halsey, William F., 227-28, 241
Hammond, Percy, 37
Harburg, "Yip," 179
Hard to Handle, 89-90
Harlow, Jean, 67
Hayes, Joan, 175
Hays, Will, 73, 86
Hayworth, Rita, 154
Heindorf, Ray, 172
Hellinger, Mark, 150
Hepburn, Katharine, 188
Herald Tribune, New York, 37, 91, 92, 96, 106, 112-13, 129, 150, 170-71, 208
Herbert, Hugh, 32
Here Comes the Navy, 97
He Was Her Man, 96
Hollywood Victory Caravan, 180-81
Hollywood Victory Committee, 179
Holt, Paul, 135, 148, 198
Hoover, J. Edgar, 106
Hope, Bob, 182, 211, 241
Houlihan, "Pickie," 16
House Un-American Activities Committee, 146
Hunter College, 25, 128
Huston, Walter, 130, 161, 188

I'd Rather Be Right, 158, 163, 164
Inness, Jill, 233
Ireland, Cagney's visit to, 221-25
Irish in Us, The, 109-110
"Irish Mafia," 108, 155, 181, 244

Ivers, Robert, 220
I Was a Fugitive from a Chain Gang, 93

Jaffe, Ada, 33
Jaffe, Sam, 33
Jaffe Troupe, 33
Jazz Singer, The, 41
Jenkins, Allen, 30-31, 90, 153
Jessel, George, 159
Jimmy the Gent, 95-96
Johnny Come Lately, 176, 177-78, 179, 183, 186
Johnny Got His Gun, 143
Johnny Vagabond (England), 183
John Paul Jones, 137
Jolson, Al, 41-42, 84, 143, 169, 217
Jolson Story, The, 169
Joseph, Edmund, 162
Journal American, New York, 133, 217

Karloff, Boris, 220
Kazan, Elia, 154
Keeler, Ruby, 94, 95
Keighley, William, 41, 149
Keith's Eighty-sixth Street Theater, 27-28
Kelly, George, 39-40
Kent, William, 30
Kilian, Victor, 35-36
Kirstein, Lincoln, 96-97
Kiss Tomorrow Goodbye, 202-3
Klein, Artie, 16
Klinger, Michael, 235
Knute Rockne, 92
Koo, Mrs. V. K. Wellington, 169
Kuniyuki, Elizabeth, 199
Kuniyuki, Kenneth, 199-200
Kunz, Roy, 98-99

Lady Killer, 95
La Guardia, Fiorello, 170
Lahr, Bert, 181
Lamarr, Hedy, 137
Larceny Lane (Blonde Crazy), 70
Lardner, Ring, 161
Lasky, Jesse, 84
Latimer, Ross F. (Kim Spaulding), 204
Laughton, Charles, 127, 144
La Verne, Lucille, 60, 61
Lawrence, Gertrude, 143, 182
Lederer, Francis, 144
Leech, John R., 144-45
Lejeune, C. A., 171
Lemmon, Jack, 210-11, 225, 241

Lenox Hill Settlement House, 23, 25
Leslie, Joan, 161, 165, 166
Levey, Ethel, 165
Levinson, Nathan, 172
Levy, Pete, 16
Lindsay, Margaret, 106
Lion Is in the Streets, A, 205
Little Caesar, 64, 66, 69
Lloyd, Roy R., 38
Lost in the Stratosphere, 71
Lost Silk Hat, The, 25
Love Me or Leave Me, 207-9, 216, 240, 241
Lux Radio Theater, 143
Lyceum, 26, 74
Lyles, A. C., 220, 236, 238, 245, 247

McAllister, Neil, 101, 102
McCrea, Joel, 178
McDaniel, Hattie, 176
McHugh, Frank, 88, 94, 107, 108, 109, 119, 149, 180, 244
MacLaine, Shirley, 241
MacRae, Gordon, 202, 204
Maggie the Magnificent, 39-41
Main, Marjorie, 176
Malone, Dorothy, 219
Manchester *Guardian*, 224
Mankiewicz, Joseph L., 19
Manners, Dorothy, 235
Man of a Thousand Faces, 218-20, 225
March, Fredric, 125, 144-45, 146
Margrave, Seton 133
Martha (yacht), 117, 127, 140, 180, 190
Martha's Vineyard, farm at, 116-17, 121, 124, 130-31, 134, 192, 212, 226, 245
Martin, Dorothy, 97
"Mary," 165, 167, 211
Mary Ann (yacht), 204
Massey, Raymond, 203
Mayer, Louis B., 159
Mayo, Virginia, 195, 202
Mayor of Hell, 93
MGM, 71, 159, 207, 216
Midsummer Night's Dream, A, 110-13
Miller, Jean, 144
Millionaire, The, 62-63, 207
Mister Roberts, 210-11, 218, 225
Mitchell, Cameron, 208
Montgomery, Robert, 175, 202, 218, 227, 228
Morgan, Dennis, 178
Morgan, Frank, 107, 108

Morning Telegraph, New York, 204
Morning World, New York, 39
Motion Picture Herald, 170
Motion Picture Producers Association, 86
Movie censors, 68-69, 73, 135-36, 138, 203
Mrs. Miniver, 172
Muni, Paul, 144
Murphy, George, 107, 175
Murray, Don, 225
Mutiny on the Bounty, 127
My Fair Lady, 235

National Film Theatre (London), 224, 225
Nelson, Gene, 202
Never Steal Anything Small, 221
New Theater (magazine), 75
New York City, 128; Lower East Side, 12; Yorkville, 14-16, 20, 26, 77, 78, 132, 241-42
New York Film Critics' Award, 133-34
New York Patrolmen's Benevolent Association, 68
New York Times, The, 40, 61, 69, 93, 95, 103, 153-54, 168, 170, 174, 178, 198, 202, 216, 220, 221-22, 227
Night Nurse, 71
Novarro, Ramon, 101

Oberon, Merle, 180
O'Biyle, Johnny, 184
O'Brien, Edmond, 196-97, 198-99
O'Brien, Margaret, 182
O'Brien, Pat, 92, 97, 104, 107, 108, 109, 110, 113-14, 119, 126, 129, 131, 132, 133, 143, 150-52, 180, 181, 244, 248
Observer, The (England), 171
Odets, Clifford, 144
Oklahoma Kid, The, 134-35, 206
O'Mara, "Brother," 16
O'Neill, Eugene, 36, 158, 191
One, Two, Three, 228-30, 231
On Your Toes, 137
Original Nut Club, 26
Oscar awards. *See* Academy Awards
Other Men's Women, 61
"Out of Town Papers," 32
Outside Looking In, 36-37
Overman, Lynne, 107, 108
"Over There," 158, 164
Over the Wall, 116

254 · INDEX

Parker, Dorothy, 128
Parker, Thelma, 34
Parker, Rand, and Cagney, 34, 95
Parsons, Louella, 65
Payton, Barbara, 203
Pelswick, Rose, 133
Penny Arcade, 41-42, 60, 217
Peralto, Ingela, 234
Perkins, Osgood, 39
Perry, Harvey, 78
Phantom President, The, 156, 158
Pickford, Mary, 83, 173
Picture Snatcher, 90-92
Pidgeon, Walter, 175
Pitter Patter, 30-31
Playboy of the Western World, 119
Pluck of the Irish, The (England), 123
Post, New York, 156, 177
Potter, H. C. ("Hank"), 191-92
Powell, Dick, 94, 110
Powell, William, 210
"Professional Againster," 79, 94, 120, 126, 243
Public Enemy, The, 63-70, 195

Queen for a Day, 214, 215
Quinlivan, "Loggerhead," 16

Radio, 123, 142-43, 174
Radio Actors Guild, 143
Raft, George, 75, 103-4, 137, 148-49
Raftery, Edward, 166
Rathbun, Stephen, 39
Reagan, Ronald, 129, 241, 245
Redgrave, Sir Michael, 221
"Red Squad," 98
Reinhardt, Max, 110-11, 112
Ritz Girls, 32
Rivkin, Alan, 90
Roaring Twenties, The, 150
Roberts, Ben, 194
Robinson, Edward G., 38, 66, 69, 70, 154, 229, 236
Rochester (Eddie Anderson), 187
Roemehld, Heinz, 172
Rogers, Ginger, 182, 187
Roman, Ruth, 204
Rooney, Mickey, 110, 112, 159, 182
Roosevelt, Franklin D., 163, 187-88
Rose, Jack, 211
Rubin, Daniel, 38
Run for Cover, 72, 206, 209
Russell, Rosalind, 187

St. Juan, Olga, 199
St. Louis Kid, 104
Saroyan, William, 190, 191, 192
Scott, George C., 241
Screen Actors Guild, 100, 175, 182
Screenland magazine, 92
Segal, George, 241
Sergel, Jack, 199-200
Seven Little Foys, The, 211
Shake Hands with the Devil, 221-23, 225
Shakespeare, William, 110-12
Sheridan, Ann, 131, 152, 153-54
Sherman, Arthur, 86
Sherman, Lowell, 35, 136
Short Cut to Hell, 220-21
Show Business at War, 182
Sidney, Sylvia, 186-87
Sight and Sound, 135
Sign, The (monthly), 174
Sign on the Door, The, 35
Sinatra, Frank, 66, 223, 238, 239, 240, 242
Singing Fool, The, 41-42
Sing Sing, prison, 26
Sinners' Holiday, 60-61
Smart Money, 70
Smith, Al, 169
Snyder, Marty "the Gimp," 207, 208
Snyder, Ruth, 90
Sobel, Louis, 217
Soldier from the Wars Returning, 218
Something to Sing About, 124
Sothern, Ann, 182
Spain, Cagney's trip to, 233-35
Spaulding, Kim (Ross F. Latimer), 204
Stanwyck, Barbara, 71, 217
Starlift, 203-4
Stars and Films, 130
Steffens, Lincoln, 99-101, 102
Sternberg, Josef von, 81
Stevens, George, Jr., 242
Strand Theater (New York), 76
Strang, W. H., 182
Strawberry Blonde, The, 154-55
Stuart, Gloria, 97
Stuyvesant High School, 19, 21-22, 230
Sullavan, Margaret, 134
Sullivan, Ed, 144, 147
Sun, New York, 19, 39
Sunday Express, London, 71, 77, 89, 95, 133, 154

Taxi, 73-76
Taylor, Mrs. William H. 69

Television, 205, 212-13, 218, 235
Temple, Shirley, 144
Theater, Cagney's start in, 36-42
Theater Guild, 38
These Wilder Years, 217
They Gave Him a Gun (England), 150
13 Rue Madeleine, 189-90
This Is Your Life, 213
Thorndike, Dame Sybil, 221
Three Comrades, 134
Tierney, Lawrence, 137
Tiffin, Pamela, 228, 229
Time magazine, 61, 89, 110, 211, 221
Time of Your Life, The, 190-92
Times, London, 186-87, 198
Times, Los Angeles, 197
Times, New York. *See New York Times, The*
Tishman, Max, 34-35, 95
Tone, Franchot, 144, 146, 175
Toomey, Regis, 106
Torrid Zone, 152
Tracy, Lee, 38, 82
Tracy, Spencer, 109, 171, 216
Tribute to a Bad Man, 216
Troy Films, 223
Truex, Ernest, 30
Trumbo, Dalton, 143
"Try-Angle, The," 34
Tucker, Sophie, 140
Twentieth Century-Fox, 118, 182
Two Orphans, The, 25
Tynan, Kenneth, 68

United Artists, 71, 83, 96, 166, 173, 176, 186, 193, 228
Universal International, 218

Velez, Lupe, 101
Variety, 34, 95, 124, 143, 187
vaudeville, 27-35, 39, 59, 248
Vernon, Billie, 31, 35. *See also* Cagney, Bill (Mrs. James Cagney)
Vernon and Nye, 31-32

Wallace, Robert, 218
Wallis, Hal, 174
Walsh, Raoul, 195, 198
Ward's Island, Cagney's visit to, 18, 195
Warner, Harry, 65, 84, 127
Warner, Jack L., 65, 72, 78-79, 80, 81, 83-84, 87, 94, 115-16, 120, 121, 122, 124, 126, 127, 142, 151, 158, 160, 161, 166, 174, 193, 243

Warner, Sam, 84
Warner Bros., 41, 59-60, 61, 64, 68, 71, 92, 105, 115, 122, 124, 129, 157, 172, 193, 208; background of, 84; and Cagney's age, 62, 178, 203; Cagney's legal battle with, 117-21, 123, 126; Cagney's relationship with, 60, 72, 78-87, 94, 114-16, 160, 193; contracts with, 60, 73, 83, 86, 113
Warner Bros.-First National, 202
Wayne, John, 178, 241
Weiss, Henri, 67
Wellman, William, 65, 67, 213
West, Mae, 118
West Point Story, The, 201-2, 218
What for Why, 25
What Price Glory?, 204
White, Alice, 90-91
White Heat, 193-98, 201
Wilder, Billy, 229
William Cagney Productions, Inc., 173, 175-76, 177, 182, 185-86, 190, 192-93, 202, 205, 208
Wilson, Marie, 129
Wilson, William, 146
Winner Take All, 77-78
Winters, Ella, 99-101
Women Go On for Ever, 38-39
Wood, Sir Kingsley, 171
Woods, Edward, 65
Woolcott, Alexander, 39
World Telegram, New York, 71, 152, 192, 217
Wycherly, Margaret, 195
Wyman, Jane, 175, 204

"Yankee Doodle Boy," 158, 160, 163, 181, 184, 211, 222
Yankee Doodle Dandy, 157-73, 174, 176, 179, 186, 193, 211, 219, 220, 225, 240, 245
Yiddish, Cagney's use of, 19, 74, 78-79, 215, 230, 235
Yorkville. *See* New York City
You, John Jones, 182
"You're a Grand Old Flag," 158, 180
Young, Captain Jack, 163
Young, Gig, 203
Young, Loretta, 74

Zanuck, Darryl, 41-42, 59-60, 65, 67, 87, 118
Zinsser, William K., 208
Zukor, Adolph, 84